WILL THAT BE ON THE FINAL?

This symbol (?) is an interrobang, said to be the first punctuation mark to enter the printed language since the quotation mark was introduced in the late 1600s.

WILL THAT BE ON THE FINAL?

By

OHMER MILTON, Ph.D.
*Director, Learning Research Center
Professor of Psychology
University of Tennessee
Knoxville, Tennessee*

CHARLES C THOMAS • PUBLISHER
Springfield • Illinois • U.S.A.

Published and Distributed Throughout the World by
CHARLES C THOMAS • PUBLISHER
2600 South First Street
Springfield, Illinois, 62717, U.S.A.

This book is protected by copyright. No part of
it may be reproduced in any manner without
written permission from the publisher.

© *1982 by* CHARLES C THOMAS • PUBLISHER
ISBN 0-398-04676-X
Library of Congress Catalog Card Number: 81-86145

With THOMAS BOOKS *careful attention is given to all details of manufacturing and design. It is the Publisher's desire to present books that are satisfactory as to their physical qualities and artistic possibilities and appropriate for their particular use.* THOMAS BOOKS *will be true to those laws of quality that assure a good name and good will.*

Printed in the United States of America
RX-10

PREFACE

AMERICANS are numbed by the numbers that are used to describe the abilities of people in general and of college students in particular. Numbers disclose and numbers distort but most of all, numbers dominate our thinking. Tests abound at every turn, and the numbers derived from all human tests, especially educational ones, should be accepted by the public with far more caution and much less grace than is presently the case.

Not only is college learning twisted by poor quality tests, but far too many life-direction decisions are based on numbers derived from classroom tests constructed hurriedly, administered carelessly, and treated cavalierly.

In all the talk and writing of the past several years about the necessity for improving college and university teaching because of unsatisfactory levels of student learning, there has been no consideration of how classroom tests contribute to either endeavor. I am convinced that better quality classroom tests are the signal route for improving teaching and the primary vehicle for enhancing learning.

My convictions are based upon: 1) careful observations of thousands of students in my classes, 2) educational research evidence accumulated over some 50 years, and 3) having witnessed my own three children's learning being compromised by tests at five separate colleges and universities.

Lest you mistakenly decide this book is a personal vendetta, I am happy to report that all of my children advanced as far as they wished; the oldest holds a Ph.D. in mathematics, the middle one earned a B.A. in English, the youngest acquired the M.D. There are many other faculty who first began to look askance at course tests when their children were victimized.

The preparation of this book has not been an academic exercise. The intent is to arouse action, that is, for outsiders—the entire panoply of students, parents, legislators, business executives, recruiters, and others—to begin to raise questions with the insiders, the professoriate, toward the end of better quality classroom tests.

These contents will provide most of the important questions which need to be asked about the substance of tests and about the numbers and letter symbols derived therefrom. Salient guidelines will be found for judging the adequacies of the answers.

O. M.

CONTENTS

	Page
Preface	v

Chapter

1. THE FOOLISH FETISH 3
2. THE MYTH OF OBJECTIVITY 17
3. INFLUENCING LEARNING 31
4. CURRENT COLLEGE TESTS 40
5. OTHER TEST FRAILTIES 52
6. WHERE TO? 69

  Notes and Acknowledgments 81
  Appendix A: Grades and Reliabilities 89
  Appendix B: Useful Books About Tests 90

WILL THAT BE ON THE FINAL?

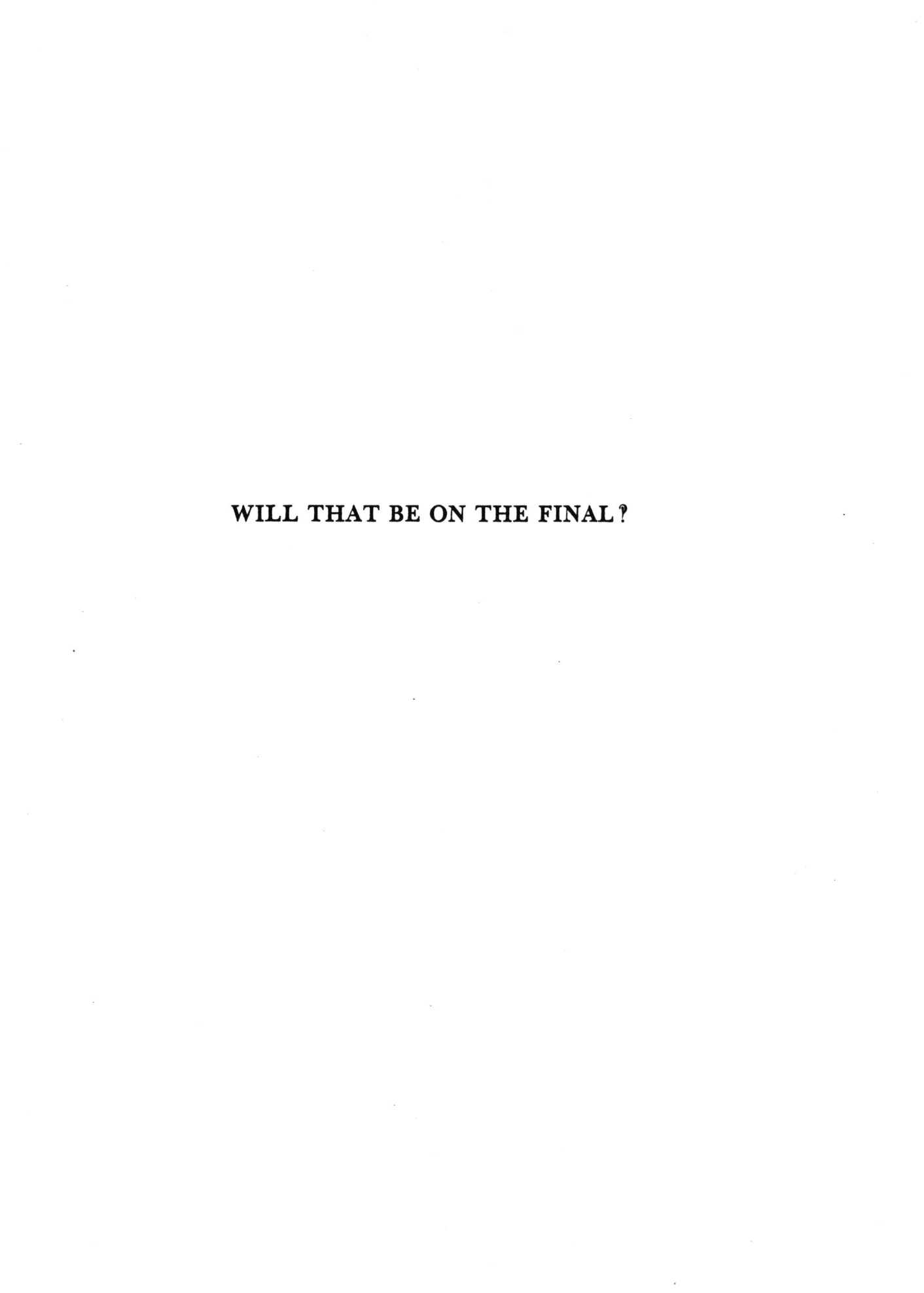

1

The Foolish Fetish

Tests have been significant facts of life throughout history and, on occasion, have been used for other than educational purposes. Around 1200 B.C., for example, the Gileadites fashioned an ingenious test as they fought the Ephramites along the shores of the Jordan River. A fugitive Ephramite, trying to cross at one of the fords, would be challenged by a Gileadite soldier with "Are you an Ephramite?" When the reply was "No," he was ordered to say "shibboleth." If the fugitive could not say the word and instead said "sibboleth," that meant he <u>was</u> an enemy Ephramite; and he was slain forthwith.

Similarly, as recently as World War II, when the Danes suspected a stranger of being a Nazi, he was directed to pronounce certain Danish words. If the suspect could not do so, the test was failed and execution was immediate.

Although college classroom tests of the late twentieth century are by no means as good quality as were those of the Gileadites and the Danes, they, too, are used for other than educational purposes. Almost as important extra-curricular decisions are made about students on the basis of classroom test scores as those that were made about enemies. Test grades, ABCD or F, are converted into numbers on permanent records; and these numbers often determine the futures of students--their continuing in college, receiving financial aid, being admitted to professional schools, getting desired jobs, and so on.

At the same time, and by some criteria most importantly, poor quality classroom tests compromise student achievement--students center on how to make the grade, oftentimes to the sacrifice of substantive learning.

In the thinking of far too many responsible professors, employers, legislators, and even students of all ages, most classroom tests are beyond reproach--with sad and generally unrecognized consequences. Such thinking promotes a complacency about, and few serious challenges of, the classroom testing enterprise in general or of the course test scores of a given student in particular. Richard Hofstadter's[1] observation provides a partial explanation for this deification of a warped process:

The American mind seems extremely vulnerable to the belief that any alleged notion which can be expressed in figures is in fact as final and exact as the figures in which it is expressed.

All the while it is most interesting, and puzzling to me, that there are periodic challenging assaults on standardized or commercial educational tests, such as those of the Educational Testing Service and of the American College Testing Program. In 1962 a carefully prepared and very thoughtful book appeared under the banner THE TYRANNY OF TESTING.[2] The author was incensed about the deleterious influences those mechanical multiple-choice tests were having upon student learning. He objected to the effort to reduce knowledge into simple all-or-none statements and to the resulting ambiguities which were especially unfair to good students.

It is my impression that the message of the book was all but ignored, and certainly there has been no application of the message to college classroom tests. If anything, the quality of these is worsening rather than improving.

The book, THEY SHALL NOT PASS,[3] appearing at about the same time, examined the intense competition swirling around high school graduates seeking admission to private colleges and universities and criticized the central role of standardized tests in the process.

There was a ten- or twelve-year period of silence, extending from the early sixties until the mid-seventies, surrounding these published tests; at that time Ralph Nader began to attack the products of the Educational Testing Service. This organization is often attractive to attackers because it is the largest test creator and publisher and also because it is the best known via the Scholastic Aptitude Test for high school students and via the Medical College Aptitude Test and the Law School Aptitude Test for students bound for professional schools. These three are known more commonly as the SAT or the College Boards, the MCAT, and the LSAT.

By the late seventies the furor had caused legislation, referred to as "Truth in Testing," to be introduced in the Congress of the United States; and several state legislatures had begun to be active along the same lines. In 1979 stringent legislation curbing commercial tests was passed in New York State. As this is being written, attacking articles are flourishing and another book blast has appeared -- THE TESTING TRAP.[4] It criticizes mechanical tests at all levels beginning with those used in the early grades and continues on to those for college and professional schools as well as licensing and Civil Service examinations.

In the meantime classroom tests continue to reign supreme; it is as though they are error free. My argument is that they, not the commercial tests, should be the primary targets of criticism. College-level standardized tests tend to be of exceptionally good quality--the purpose of each one has been conceived carefully by many thoughtful scholars; each question has been scrutinized repeatedly and at length for both intent and clarity; and the final effort is tested (in much the same fashion as cars are at proving grounds) before being released to the public.

I have had personal experience in helping to construct these tests, and I know the time and care which are invested in the creation of each question. Furthermore, astronomical numbers of college students are affected by poor quality classroom tests almost daily -- in contrast to the few who are affected annually by standardized ones. But it is not my intention to defend these tests or to make a brief for their use; rather I wish to redirect test criticisms.

With approximately ten million students in colleges and universities today and each one carrying three courses (conservatively) per term and having two tests on the average in each course, some 60 million classroom tests are given every three or four months--for a total of close to 200 million in an academic year. By stark contrast only one or two million standardized tests are given to college students during a comparable period of time.

Even though my arithmetic may be in error by several million, the numbers are nonetheless staggering. To emphasize my point with numbers that can be comprehended readily, a given student during four years of college **will** take 120 classroom tests at the least (two tests in each of 15 courses per year) and **might** take two or three standardized ones.

Perhaps standardized tests are the primary targets of criticism because, in some instances, important decisions are made about students on the basis of the scores. What is forgotten is that important decisions are made much more often on the basis of classroom test scores--and that both types of scores are abused frequently by those who should know better.

The assumption must be that a few awry scores among the 100 or so garnered during a college career will not matter a great deal; they will average out. But a difference of one one-hundredth of a point-- 2.99 versus 3.00, for example--in a grade-point-average (derived from classroom test scores) can determine whether or not a student is considered for a job or for admission to a professional school such as law or medicine.

Surely one of the reasons for the revived attacks on standardized tests is the increased competition for jobs and for admission to certain professional schools--in particular, medicine. And competition for admission to prestigious private colleges and universities seems to be continuing unabated. Again, grades (as was true for admission to private colleges in the early sixties), not standardized test scores, receive the most weight; that is, grades are still the most important admissions criterion. This assertion has been documented by a major study[5] conducted under the auspices of the College Entrance Examination Board and the American

Association of Collegiate Registrars and Admission Officers (I refuse to reduce these titles to acronyms). I suspect that high school tests are no better than college ones.

Strangely, there is silence about the quality of the so-called competency tests--those that the states are requiring students to pass before being allowed to graduate from high school. My friends around the nation tell me that some of these tests are sorely deficient. I suppose these state prepared tests are appealing to the public because the numbers derived therefrom presumably prove accountability. We are numbed by the numbers. (The guidelines for quality classroom tests are equally suitable for these competency ones).

Before some recruiters from business and industry visit a campus, they specify that they wish to interview students who have a given GPA, or above. And medical schools make it clear that students with GPA's below a certain level need not apply.

About the only criticism classroom testing receives is highly indirect; for the past decade or so the criticism has been manifested in a disguised way by alarm over grade inflation. Studies and articles about the phenomenon abound. In my view, though, grades and grade inflation are only symptoms. Classroom tests are the malignancies; it is the several questions in each one of them which compromise learning in a number of ways (see Chapter 3).

To deviate from generalizations for just a moment, here is a question that was used in a junior-level course very recently; it was one of several in a 50-minute exam:

> Since we know how bad inflation is, why is it that we are not now, and have not since 1972, brought inflation rates down to acceptable levels?

The intent of the professor who wrote this question may have been beyond reproach (but I doubt it!)--encouraging students to reason, to be critical, to order their thoughts, to write clearly--but this is a bad, a poor-quality question. I hope the reasons for my sharp judgment shine through by the end of the book.

Lest you conclude I'm singling out essay questions for damnation, here is a poor-quality multiple-choice one from a sophomore course:

Amicus curiae refers to:

a) the grounds for revocation of bail

b) someone offering advice to the court, though not actually a party to the case under consideration

c) Congressional limitations upon the Court's jurisdiction

d) a judge removing himself from a case because of a conflict of interest

The test-sharp student who has no idea about the meaning of the term "amicus curiae" but knows the test-taking tricks picks alternative "b" immediately.

This true-false item from a senior course is most expressive of both substance and quality and is a direct contribution to grade inflation:

Fiscal policy influences economic activity in the economy!!

It is my guess that as you read, you will recall many of your own experiences with college tests. For example, I remember true-false test questions in a graduate statistics course, many of which came from textbook footnotes. More than likely you were exposed to tests during the time, between 1950 and now, when their use became alarmingly twisted. As a consequence, your views of them are limited -- thus a few reminders.

Purposes

What are the purposes of classroom testing? There are two major ones. Ideally tests assist in the promotion of learning; test results serve as means of informing both students and the teacher whether or not the students have learned in that particular course. If they have not, proper help can be provided.

Assistance should include detailed criticisms and suggestions; for example, "'None are' is incorrect -- 'none' requires the singular verb 'is'." "'The woman that' is wrong -- this reference to a person requires the personal pronoun 'who'; never matter what you are hearing on television"; "'different than' is incorrect -- 'different from' is correct." Tests help detect errors of omission and commission in the performance of students.

Although the importance of specific constructive criticism, along with approval and encouragement for improving learning, seems to be well known by all who have taught informally (our own children, for instance), its use in most college classrooms is almost non-existent. For verification of that assertion, ask a few students. Just why college teachers are reluctant to praise or criticize is a bit of a mystery; praise and criticism are useful -- indeed essential -- in correcting ignorance. (Yes, I used "ignorance" quite intentionally, it cannot be eliminated simply by banning the term.)

Research in the schools has demonstrated the potency of knowledge of results, as psychologists call it (or feedback); it can take several forms. As illustrations, one of the best studies was conducted in 74 classrooms.[6] Learning was enhanced for those students who received appropriate personal comments on their papers -- "Excellent," "Good work," "That's fine," "Try to do still better," "You can make it," and others.

In another well-executed investigation,[7] students for whom answers to questions on corrected test papers were discussed by the instructor performed better on subsequent tests than did students for whom there had been no discussion. In still another study, college students who received no information about the correctness of their answers to multiple-choice questions tended to remember incorrect answers rather than correct ones.[8]

Several years ago a group of investigators[9] corrected English themes by dictating on tapes. Students then used playback machines which were located in the library. Listening to corrections seemed much more significant and palatable to students than reading them had been. With this equipment becoming increasingly inexpensive, more of this ought to be tried. Finally, the computer is being used to provide feedback in a genetics course; performance on problem solving questions is enhanced.[10]

Knowledge of results need not be verbal; facial expressions and nods or shaking of the head convey important messages. Personally tailored feedback might assist students in learning to provide their own; for most of us, following graduation, our only detailed tutors and critics will be ourselves.

Many, many times students have test papers returned with only a lone letter, ABCD or F, on the front; there are no corrections or comments thereon. This is not feedback for the serious student. Most scoring machines make no marks, even whether a given answer is right or wrong. In still other instances, test papers are not returned; this is particularly true for final exams.

One of the reasons college athletes improve their skills -- that is, learn to play better -- is that coaches observe them carefully, call incorrect actions to their attention, and show them how to make corrections. Some coaches praise and encourage; others condemn and berate; and still others mix the two approaches. The point is that help is detailed and personal for each player; these are some of the reasons that coaches are among the nation's best teachers. Most of us could profit from observing them during practice sessions. A football coach remarked: "I take an exam every Saturday afternoon."

One does not have to be engaged in formal teaching to recognize the significance of the feedback principle. Did you know that the "ringing" of the other telephone after you dial is fake? How would you feel if there were only silence? And why is there a light under an elevator button? Only to provide feedback when you push it. Note, too, that the turn signals on your car when activated produce both clicks and flashing lights on the dashboard. We need to know the consequences of our actions; the importance of this principle cannot be overemphasized.

In reality, the other major purpose of testing and the one receiving the most attention decidedly is to cull, sort, rank-order, and classify students. They are graded prime, choice, good, and commercial. Colleges and universities have become personnel-selection agencies for society. In this context grades are mostly for record-keeping purposes, and these records are for sharing with others--employers and graduate and professional school officials. Students are keenly aware of this function; and many, if not most, of them are concerned only about the grade -- theirs is the symbol scramble!

I used to give students in my classes the opportunity to choose between having their test papers discussed in detail or only receiving their grades; around three-fourths chose the latter. Many faculty members know of this single-minded symbol scramble, and so a vicious circle develops-- faculties affect students negatively, and vice versa. There are circular effects.

Students are not alone in seeking the symbols; their parents are often allies and sometimes to their chagrin, as revealed in this letter[11] from a coed:

Dear Mother and Dad:
   Since I left for college, I have been remiss in writing and am sorry for my thoughtlessness in not having written before. I will bring you up to date now; but before you read on, please sit down.
   Well, then, I am getting along pretty well now. The skull fracture and the concussion I got when I jumped out of the window of my dormitory when it caught on fire shortly after my arrival here is pretty well healed now. I can see almost normally, and only get those sick headaches once a day. Fortunately, the fire in the dormitory, and my jump, was witnessed by an attendant at the gas station near the dorm; and he was the one who called the Fire Department and the ambulance. He also visited me in the hospital; and since I had nowhere to live because of the burnt-out dormitory, he was kind enough to invite me to share his apartment with him. It's really a basement room, but it's kind of cute. He is a very fine boy and we have fallen deeply in love and are planning to get married. We haven't set the exact date yet, but it will be before my pregnancy begins to show.

Yes, Mother and Dad, I am pregnant. I know how much you are looking forward to being grandparents, and I know you will welcome the baby and give it the same love and devotion and tender care you gave me when I was a child. The reason for the delay in our marriage is that my boy friend has a minor infection which prevents him from passing our pre-marital blood tests, and I carelessly caught it from him.

I know that you will welcome him into our family with open arms. He is kind and, although not well educated, he is ambitious.

Now that I have brought you up to date, I want to tell you that there was no dormitory fire; I did not have a concussion or skull fracture; I was not in the hospital; I am not pregnant; I am not engaged; I am not infected; and there is no boy friend in my life. However, I am getting a D in History and an F in Chemistry, and I want you to see those marks in their proper perspective.

Your loving daughter,
Susie

Sorting, rank-ordering, and classifying mean that students are being compared one against another, or against some very vague professorial standard. It is for these reasons that the devices or tests on which grades are based should be constructed with great care and corrected with as much fairness as can be mustered. This theme will be elaborated as we go along. And while I disapprove of this sorting practice, the odds are very high it will continue. Indeed, the Buckley Amendment, which allows students access to their records, seems to be contributing to this continuation. This law allows students to see their records -- consequently letters of recommendation and other non-test documents are more and more innocuous. Since the sorting practice will continue, all features of it ought to be improved.

Many of you know that letter grades are converted into quality points; in most schools an A is weighted 4, a B 3, and so on. To refresh your memory a bit, all courses carry a specified number of credit hours. A grade of A for a 3-hour course would result in 12 quality points; a grade of B in the same course would equal 9 points, and so on. To obtain the haloed grade-point average (GPA), all the points are added and that total is divided by the total number of credit hours. But watch it! The weights are different at some schools--an A is weighted 3, a B 2, a C 1. A GPA from one of these will be drastically different.

What is not known is that the GPA is a meaningless statistic. I am quite aware of the computational machinations employed to try to make a given GPA mean something. But as students put it, "Garbage in, Garbage out." True or False -- "Fiscal policy influences economic activity in the economy." All numbers must have referents to be interpreted. Where oh where are those within GPA's?

Although the central theme of this book is about tests and not about the symbols, here is a good place to attempt once more to dispel some of the myths about grades, to try to clear the air, to make the gesture, so that the most significant problem, the fundamental problem, -- test quality -- can be addressed.

There has been uncritical acceptance of the notion that grades and grade averages are good or excellent indicators of future performance or achievement. I have found in discussions with others and following formal addresses about tests to sophisticated audiences that it is all but impossible to keep the focus on the main topic; inevitably the debates return to grades. To repeat, grades are surface issues.

I must confess that reason seems to have little to do with dispelling myths. As George Bernard Shaw once observed:

> There is no harder scientific fact in the world than the fact that belief can be produced in practically unlimited quantity and intensity, without observation or reasoning, and even in defiance of both by the simple desire to believe founded on a strong interest in believing.

Francis Bacon[12] recognized this truth centures ago when he observed:

> In the year of our Lord 1432, there arose a grievous quarrel among the brethren over the number of teeth in the mouth of a horse. For 13 days the disputation raged without ceasing. All the ancient books and chronicles were fetched out, and wonderful and ponderous erudition, such as was never before heard of in this region, was made manifest. At the beginning of the 14th day, a youthful friar of goodly bearing asked his learned superiors for permission to add a word, and straight-away, to the wonderment of the disputants, whose deep wisdom he sore vexed, he beseeched them to unbend in a manner coarse and unheard-of, and to look in the open mouth of a horse and find the answer to their questionings. At this, their dignity being grievously hurt, they waxed exceedingly wroth; and, joining in a mighty uproar, they flew upon him and smote him hip and thigh, and cast him out forthwith. For, said they, surely Satan hath tempted this bold neophyte to declare unholy and unheard-of ways of finding truth contrary to the teachings of the fathers. After many days of grievous strife, the dove of peace sat on the assembly, and they as one man, declaring the problem to be an everlasting mystery because of a grievous dearth of historical and theological evidence thereof, so ordered the same writ down.

Perhaps we faculty created the myth; most of us had high GPA's and quite obviously reached the zeniths of intellectual attainment (according to certain observers). Our own high college grades are one of the reasons we cling to the myth of the mighty GPA.

The facts of the matter are that grades do not predict future accomplishments or post-college achievements with any reasonable degree of accuracy; they are not good indicators of future performance. That is, students who are graduated with C averages are about as likely to achieve as well as are students who are graduated with A averages. Many of the studies which support that assertion have been brought together in a careful review;[13] here are brief descriptions of two of the best ones.

One of them involved 10,000 employees of the American Telephone and Telegraph Company in the early 1960's. It was found that 45 percent of the employees who had been graduated in the top third of their classes earned salaries which were in the top third. But at the same time, 25 percent of the lower third academically earned salaries in the top third. (It is well known that salary is not always an accurate reflection of ability or performance-- each of you will attest to this verity.)

A well known researcher took me to task once before an audience of at least 300 psychologists when I cited this study. It developed that he had not read it. Such is the emotional power of grades--we are numbed by the numbers.

The other study was an elaborate and refined series of investigations of 426 Utah physicians; 102 full-time medical faculty members of the University of Utah; 109 board-qualified specialists; 110 urban general practitioners; 105 rural small-town general practitioners. Over 200 measures of on-the-job performance were collected carefully for each physician.

It was found that academic achievement--both undergraduate and medical school--was unrelated to those features of the practice of medicine. To put it another way for the statistically minded readers, course grades did not correlate with the certain specifics in the practice of medicine.

A very renowned college professor was jarred when he contrasted what the top eight college students were doing as graduates with what eight really poor students were doing.[14] Around 15 years out of school, there were teachers, physicians, lawyers, and scientists in both groups. The difference was that those with the top undergraduate grades had been allowed to attend the prestigious graduate and professional schools.

In another especially damning study, EDUCATION AND JOBS: THE GREAT TRAINING ROBBERY,[15] it was demonstrated that there is little relationship between formal education and on-the-job performance. Prominent officials in major industries were emphatic, however, in declaring that the good qualities of young workers had accrued to them because they had been through four years of college. Without any evidence to support their actions, the officials used the diploma to screen out those they considered undesirables. The most recently marshalled evidence against the predictive validity of grades appeared in 1975 in a study conducted for the United States Civil Service Commission.[16]

It is especially regrettable that faculties think no more clearly about these matters than does the public. In this connection a favorite faculty sport is that of toying with grade-point-averages, usually for the presumed cause of raising standards. Periodically, the composition of the GPA is altered. If a course is repeated, should both grades or only the last one go into the computations? Should grades transferred from other schools be counted? How should Incompletes be weighted? And on and on! Nothing is ever said about how the grades were derived in the first place or about the quality of the tests upon which they are based.

A well-executed survey[17] of around 500 colleges and universities in 1975 documented the fact that there are unbelievable variations in grade recording and GPA calculation practices from school to school. Yet most of the local eccentricities are not described on the transcripts of a given institution. An A is an A is an A. Such indifferentations mean that GPA's from different schools <u>cannot</u> be compared directly; obviously they are and with abandon!

Numbers tend to numb the thinking of many of us. The transcript practice which reflects this and that disturbs me most of all is the almost universal failure to make any distinctions between an academic F and an administrative F. An administrative F goes on a student's transcript, for example, when the Registrar is not notified that a course has been dropped. And in all too many instances, it remains, despite valiant efforts to remove it. Is it any wonder that grades are poor indicators of post-college performance?

Another reason for grades being poor predictors of the future is the fact that they are uni-dimensional symbols into which multi-dimensional phenomena have been forced. A final grade can be based upon how a student scored on course tests as well as attitude toward the course, promptness in meeting assignments, attendance, class contributions, and others. Some faculty consider almost all of these; other faculty consider only a few, while still others consider only test performance. There is no way of determining the proportion of the ingredients in the great mix after the symbol leaves the psyche of the professor.[18]

Furthermore, there are several letter grading systems, that is, the standards or guidelines individual faculty members use in assigning letter grades. The different systems are employed on the same campus and in the same academic departments. Four of these systems were found in operation at the University of Washington.[19]

Absolute -- a specified number of points is necessary for each letter grade. For example, 95-100=A, 85-94=B, and so on. Even when these levels are detailed in a catalogue, they are not followed by all faculty. The point levels vary, even from course to course, and certainly from school to school. Fifty-one percent of the faculty used this standard.

Inspection -- the entire array of scores for a class is rank-ordered and then examined for breaks or gaps; the gaps determine the different grade levels. For example, several students obtain scores of 87 or higher; the next highest score is 84 and another group of scores cluster between 79 and 84. All students with 87 and higher receive A's; those with scores between 79 and 84 receive B's. Thirty percent of the faculty used this guideline.

Normal curve -- this is the familiar "grading on the curve"; it is not a normal curve because most faculty and students do not know that the "normal curve" is a mathematical abstraction. Nevertheless a certain percentage in a class receive A's, a higher percentage receive B's; the percentages of A's and F's will be roughly the same as will the percentages of B's and D's. This standard was used by 12 percent of the faculty.

Individual -- progress of the student is judged rather than attainment of course content. This one was used by only seven percent of the faculty.

These different systems add up to the fact that a given level of attainment can result in any of the letter grades! Were all of these standards used in assigning your college grades? Did you know at the time which ones were being used? The answer to the first question is certainly "Yes" and to the second probably "No."

Sometimes there is no relation between the level of achievement and the grade assigned, and any of the standards can be distorted in unimagined ways:

A student with the highest overall point total in her class (90) received a B rather than an A as her final grade. The instructor explained that his point system was absolute and that while she had a "moral A," he could not give her an A for the course. During the conversation, he told her he had given another student a B when that student had only enough points for a C. He rationalized that there was a difference between giving someone a B and giving someone an A but did not explain what the difference was.

In a formal study at a dental school, 20 faculty members were asked to make brief comments about student performance along with assigning the grade. Study the results in this table carefully:

Student	Grade	Comment
#1	B	Poor x-ray to show buccal canal, trial points too long
#2	B	Well done, rare
#3	B	Student needs a lot of help, is not certain of essential concept.
#4	C+	Student did very well, knew what he had to do and did it.
#5	C	Well filled root canal, competent performance
#6	C	This student is too meticulous
#7	C	Cautious

Comments by me about these absurdities are not necessary other than to say they are not atypical. Remember: only the letter grade for a course goes on the transcript and becomes part of the permanent record and of the GPA. Is it any wonder the GPA is a meaningless statistic?

In addition, what are the net effects of juggling and averaging symbols which have come from questions such as this one, asked of seniors, along with questions of good quality? One needs a college course to answer:

An individual should secure the assistance of a _____ when preparing a will.

Before a transcript is released to anyone outside the college or university, all the GPA numbers should be removed. Any who wished to calculate averages would then know the composition of them!!

There are marked parallels between faculties toying with GPA's and Congress toying with income tax reforms; both bodies refuse to address malignancies. Inequities are piled upon inequities, and unfairness escalates. There is one important difference--most of us know that the income tax irregularities are present, but either we do not know about GPA eccentricities, or we choose to ignore them.

The sanctity of the averages reminds me, too, of first-down measurements in football. Officials have the impossible task of placing the ball on the ground with the same preciseness from tackle to tackle. But as short a distance as less than an inch, as measured by the chain, is final and exact. Watch the care and precision with which the chains are manipulated and watch the official on television holding his hands up to indicate the tiny distance out of 100 yards by which the first down was missed.

I see no way of resolving grading--ABCD or F--issues and problems! But if faculties can be reached, the tests upon which grades are based can be improved. Thus, one straightforward, but neglected, route to improvement of the evaluation enterprise is that of improving classroom tests--without fail, the cause of learning will be improved! Presently neither of the major purposes of classroom tests is being fulfilled properly.

2

The Myth of Objectivity

Discussions and debates about classroom tests invariably center around the question of whether they should be subjective or objective. This limited and misleading concern about tests began around 1915 following several studies[1] in history, English, and mathematics in which it was found that the marking of test papers tended to be highly variable. This finding has been verified and refined by numerous subsequent investigations; a given paper tends to be marked differently by two different teachers--and even differently by the same teacher on separate occasions.

Another early classic along these lines was conducted in England.[2] The history papers of 15 students, each containing answers to six questions, were given to 15 examiners; and each examiner was asked to grade each one independently on a three-level scale. There were wide discrepancies among the grades assigned, and more than half the students both passed and failed.

A year later the examiners were asked, without having received advanced notice, to mark the papers again; these grades differed significantly from the original ones. Similar variations were found in marking Latin, French, English, and chemistry papers.

A few moments' reflection will suggest several very plausible explanations for these variations in marking. Using mathematics papers as examples, one teacher might ignore minor arithmetic errors and be concerned only with the method by which a problem is solved; another teacher scoring the same papers might have opposite concerns. More than likely, grades assigned by the two would be different. I used this example deliberately because so many get upset by believing that mathematics is so exact. As for different grades by the same teacher, early-morning grading, when one is fresh and rested, might vary from grading in the late evening when one is worn out mentally and physically.

Compounding these rather obvious explanations is the fact that many college teachers are not too clear in their own thinking about their aims in teaching; as a consequence, they vacillate and do so without informing students of their changes in direction.

Nevertheless, over the years the erroneous conclusion was reached by many mental measurement experts that essay papers cannot be scored fairly or consistently--and therefore must not be used. Essay questions were labeled subjective and came to be thought of as bad. The facts are that essay or subjective questions <u>can</u> be marked fairly and consistently.

History

In the meantime, shortly after the initial studies, a new type test was developed for use during World War I. There were two forms, one for readers and one for non-readers; on either form the soldier chose among predetermined answers to questions--and here were the propelling origins of the standardized, or commercial, tests which are under attack today.

These new tests were labeled "objective"; anyone could correct them at any time, any place, <u>after</u> the scoring key was prepared, and arrive at identical results. Therefore, went the reasoning, these tests were good.

In some circles the tests were labeled scientific; this appellation adds further unwarranted goodness. It is significant to note that it was at this time, some 60 years ago, that the quality of tests began to be judged by the experts almost entirely on the basis of the consistency of marking or scoring. The substance seemed to be of little moment.

The major purpose of these World War I tests was that of classifying several hundred thousand men for different types of training and soldiering. Psychologists, who were the leaders in devising the tests, were ecstatic because they derived such large numbers of scores to manipulate statistically--and all this before the days of computers or even hand-cranked calculators. For some professors the statistics became more important than the contents of the tests. It must be emphasized that this type test was so useful because very large numbers of men had to be processed or classified in very short periods of time.

During the late twenties and into the thirties, these objective or mechanical tests began to be used in elementary and high schools and also in colleges. World War II brought further development and improvement of the tests, and not thousands, but many millions of young people were tested. Again the purpose was to classify recruits and volunteers in very short periods of time to place them in the most appropriate slots.

Psychologists went wild because they had not millions but billions of numbers to correlate and otherwise juggle; now they were aided by desk electric calculators. Their proclivities toward eventually substituting numbers for judgment were enhanced. I hope this book will help to head off what might happen now that computers are commonplace.

Just after World War II, in the late forties and early fifties, these new tests invaded college and university classrooms on a grand scale, first because of the large numbers of veterans who hit suddenly. Note how the purpose of objective tests changed from sorting young people in war time to measuring their learning in peace time. These functions strike me as being diametrically opposites.

It was during this immediate post-World War II period that the personnel-selection function of higher education gathered encompassing momentum, along with a screening-them-out philosophy. Introductory courses overflowed, and many veterans did not possess the usually expected attributes. As the veteran population waned, it became more and more socially desirable to attend college; as a consequence, enrollments continued to swell. Harassed faculty saw objective test questions as simple routes to testing--the questions were easy (!) to write, and papers could be corrected by clerks or student assistants.

All the while there were important national demands for highly educated people--scientists of all types, dentists, physicians, lawyers, faculty members, and others. Fierce competition for graduate and professional students developed among the specialists.

The birth rate had been very depressed from around 1930 until around 1942. A youngster born in 1932, for example, turned 18, the usual college entering age, in 1950. Thus the supply of college graduates (for advanced study) was to remain scarce until the late sixties.

Another pressure was Sputnik and the predictable American penchant to blame the schools for all social problems and to demand panaceas as instant solutions. In the meantime, textbook publishers began providing objective test questions to accompany their wares; we'll return to this topic.

With this multitude of forces impinging upon us, we tended to forget that the ideal purpose of testing is to aid the cause of learning and that one ideal purpose of a college or university is to promote student learning. As we enter the eighties, student populations on most campuses will be anything but white 18-21-year-olds. Already older females, as one illustration, are attending in large numbers. Will our testing practices continue to be primarily rank-ordering and sorting ones? It is not unusual for institutional arrangements to survive well beyond their usefulness-- you've heard the old saw "We've always done it that way".

Most faculty members receive no formal instruction in the craft they practice--even most of those who serve as teaching assistants while in graduate school learn by trial and error without systematic supervision. Since informal discussions about teaching, and about testing especially, are rare also, most of them tend to use uncritically the practices of their mentors. The vast majority of today's faculty members were undergraduates during the era of objective testing and were overexposed particularly in their introductory courses.

This means that many fundamental aspects of classroom testing have not been examined thoughtfully by most current professorial practitioners. Usually it is necessary for outsiders to force a group to examine its activities; I believe the place to start, in this instance, is with the terms "subjective" and "objective." They are misused not only by the members of the higher education establishment but by the general public as well.

Objections to Objective

I sense a general aura of good surrounding objective--a sort of halo--and a general aura of bad surrounding subjective. It is as though decisions and judgments and interpretations which we delude ourselves into thinking have been made objectively are likely to be sound, while if human or subjective elements have entered, they will be unsound. Thus one hears and reads both inside and outside the academy such expressions as:

1) Student opinions about teaching are just too subjective.
2) If only evaluations of faculty were objective, I'd agree to their use.
3) Grades should be objectively based.
4) He made a value judgment.
5) That was a subjective decision.

I hope philosophers and related scholars who peruse these words will be kind, because I know this analysis is elementary from their perspectives. I submit that neither an opinion nor an evaluation can be objective. Opinions and evaluations express internal states of the person rendering them; the essence of each is something from within an individual. Opinions and evaluations are subjective, by definition.

The first three expressions are voiced all too often by faculty members who should know better. Very similar assertions are voiced by all manner of Americans about other issues:

1) That's no way to look into a problem--you're too subjective.
2) One has to be objective about these things, you know.
3) A mark of a good business executive is objectivity.

In these days of opinion polling, it is quite common to be asked "To what extent do you agree. . .?--Strongly Agree, Agree, Disagree, Strongly Disagree." And sometimes the answers are thoughtless. Then, numbers or weights are assigned to each level, often arbitrarily and always subjectively; and then all manner of arithmetic calculations result in the name of science and objectivity.

To use the prefix "value" as a modifier for judgment as in "He made a value judgment" is the epitome of redundancy--all judgments are made within some framework of values, even though they may not be explicit. It is very amusing to hear a professor say with an air of apology, "Now I'm making a value judgment," or when one professor attacks the utterance of another with, "That was a value judgment" or to read in a leading newspaper "The human value judgment was made to . . . ." At the same time, to use the word "subjective" as in "The subjective decision was reached to . . . ." is totally unnecessary. Only people make decisions, and a decision comes from within a given individual. Only people render judgments.

Specifically:
1) A careful physician gathers information about a patient; this may include reports from laboratory tests and blood pressure readings (or test scores). These are evaluated--that is, sorted, weighed, and integrated by the physician; and a decison or judgment is made--this treatment or that treatment or no treatment. It is made within the mind, or subjectively. Values of our society and of the physician are central to the endeavor.
2) Geologists conduct many sorts of tests on the cores they remove from the earth--each test produces a number or numbers. These are interpreted and will be part of the evidence which will help them to decide to drill for oil in location X rather than in location Y. One of the values propelling them is obvious.
3) A teacher has several classroom test scores on a student. Unlike the laboratory tests of the physicians and those of the geologists, these tests are idiosyncratic and have meaning only to the teacher. The teacher's values or subjectivity entered to a marked degree when the tests were constructed--even multiple-choice ones. The teacher may interpret the scores in a variety of ways.

I am trying to suggest that in the final analysis, decisions, interpretations, and judgments--especially those teachers make about students even when using test scores--are subjective. Moreover, the assigning of grades, ABCD or F, to multiple-choice and true-false test scores is completley subjective; that is, students with scores above this point will receive A's, those with scores between here and here will receive B's, and so on. These translations of numbers into letters are arbitrary and subjective. Subjectivity in evaluation is illustrated further by the fact that experts sometimes differ among themselves as to the meaning of a given test score, be they physicians, geologists, or teachers.

Kenneth Boulding[3] has remarked:
Perhaps the greatest superstition in the world today is numerology--the belief that somehow numerical information is always superior to qualitative, structural, and topological information. The plain truth is that numbers for the most part are a figment of the human imagination . . . . There is nothing wrong with evidence as long as it is not mistaken for truth. To

believe that evidence is truth is a sure recipe for making bad decisions. Decision results from an evaluation of the evidence and a very complete weighing of alternatives. It always transcends, though it does not necesssarily reject, numerical information.

Thus to fuss about which type of test, subjective or objective, is to obfuscate and to miss the important issue--test quality. All classroom tests are subjective in one way or another. To seek objective evaluations about students is a waste of time--there are no such things! And to apologize for judgments by modifying them with "value" is to deny one's humanness as well as to disavow the meaning of the word "judgment."

As a major start toward clearer thinking about classroom tests, I suggest we cease using the word "objective." It bestows an unwarranted respectability and hides the frailties and deficiencies of those tests to which it is applied; we are deceived by the term. By not using objective, we--students, faculties, the public--will be more likely to ask the right questions about testing. The term "objective" is a deterrent to clear thinking. Let's ban its usage.

Classroom tests do not meet the several criteria which compromise the definition of objective, as contained in any good dictionary--of or having to do with a known or perceived object as distinguished from something existing only in the mind; being, or regarded as being, independent of the mind; determined by and emphasizing the features and characteristics of the object, or thing dealt with, rather than the thoughts of the writer. . . .

For all classroom tests, faculties must seek to improve the interpretative elements, that is, to minimize arbitrariness. The use of numbers and the label "objective" do not guarantee the abolition of capriciousness. The very common error of equating quantification with objectivity must be addressed more fully and completely than I have here. Determining the final score on a classroom test is only one of the several steps of the process. Faculties must develop their abilities to render considered opinions or considered judgments about students; scores from single tests and grade-point-averages can help, but they are not substitutes.

The substitution of numbers for judgment is illustrated dramatically in this very abbreviated case history.[4] Robin White, as an advanced medical student, failed Part I of the National Board Examination three times over a period of one year. Part I tests knowledge of the basic sciences; questions are of a multiple true-false variety. (I have known many excellent students who perform poorly on these mechanical tests--I do not know the explanation.)

Robin was allowed to continue her training but was advised that she could not graduate with her class. In the meantime, she passed Part II of the Boards--the clinical part--and was lauded by several faculty members for being such a good student; the prediction was made by them and by several practicing physicians who had observed her that she would be a fine doctor.

But the faculty was adamant in its position that passing Part I was a condition for graduation. With the financial help of physician friends, Robin sued the school and won; she graduated with her class.

I fear that the utilization of unexamined numbers in making decisions will get worse before it gets better. I think here of our very right concerns about abolishing racism and sexism in student affairs--grades in courses, admissions to graduate and professional schools, and so on. But we have become so accustomed to equating numbers, no matter how derived, with objectivity--when we really mean fairness and impartiality--that we may continue to hide behind numbers.

It is my impression that the courts are encouraging this hiding; court officials seem just as guilty as the rest of us in equating numbers with objectivity. Numbers are numbing because they are associated with presumed scientific accuracy and exactness in the thinking of far too many people.

I am very much aware that this is indeed a most difficult assignment; there are certainly no easy routes to its attainment. Continuing with the reliance upon numbers, though, will merely delay tackling the real problems entailed in trying to arrive at sound judgments about people.

Meanwhile, in other areas, both as individuals and as a nation, we are making progress with the meaning of numbers. We are quite cognizant of the fact that the number indicating miles-per-gallon is not sacred and fixed. Indeed, in advertising of new cars, two numbers are given: one for city driving and one for over-the-road; moreover, both are given as estimates. We now know that these numbers must be interpreted; that is, numerous factors must be considered in determining miles-per-gallon for a given car at a given time.

Three sets of factors influence miles-per-gallon: 1) the driver--type of starts made, speed, steadiness; 2) the car--condition of carburetor, points, and plugs, tire inflation, weight; 3) road and traffic conditions--frequency of stops and starts, dry or wet pavement, degree of grade, type of pavement.

Test scores of students should be given as estimates because that is exactly what they are. Three sets of factors combine to determine a student's test score: 1) the student--ability, preparedness, rested or fatigued; 2) the quality of the test--valid, reliable (discussed later in this chapter); 3) test conditions--clarity of directions, comfort of the room, lighting, noise level.

Pause now and consider how you would even get started in trying to answer this question. I don't know how to categorize it--it is neither multiple-choice nor essay! It was <u>one of several</u> on a 50-minute test for sophomores:

> Write a few lines on:
> 1) I.Q.
> 2) Evolution
> 3) The Scientific Method
> 4) Role and Status
> 5) Instinct and Learned Behavior

The real issue is making better evaluation of student learning; tests can assist in this pursuit, and the better quality they are, the better the evaluations. All types of tests (except one) can be useful, depending upon what aspects of learning a teacher wishes to tap--recognition, recall, comprehension, application, evaluation, or others.

The one exception is true-false tests; they have <u>no</u> place in the college classroom!! There is my judgment; note that I did <u>not</u> apologize for it by adding the modifier, value. It is my considered opinion.

Good quality true-false items are all but impossible to write, and to do so is inordinately time consuming. Many true-false items focus upon simple facts or trivia; this encourages rote memorization. Furthermore, the guessing element is so large that a final test score is difficult to interpret. A score of 25 can be made on a 50-item test solely by guessing.

> True-False:
> Aristotle believed that integrity was the speaker's most important attribute.
> Semantics is primarily involved with meaning.

While conducting research for this book, I found--much to my consternation--that true-false tests are used in some medical schools not only in courses but also in clinical contexts. The most flagrant example I encountered of there being no relation between learning objectives and tests was a 100-item true-false test being given to third-year students at the completion of a three-month clerkship in Internal Medicine. The purpose of the clinical experience had been for these advanced students to begin to learn to "put it all together."

I have seen true-false tests in law courses, also. Important problems in medicine and law (or in any field) seldom have clear-cut, simple, unequivocal answers. In the words of St. Augustine: "For so it is, O Lord, My God, I measure it. But what it is I measure, I do not know."

Quality

Just what is a quality classroom test? First, a quality test is one which measures what it is supposed to measure or is valid; and second, it does so fairly and dependably or is reliable! The tests of the Gileadites and Danes were both valid and reliable.

A quality test determines the extent to which students have attained the aims or objectives of the course--critical thinking in economics, problem solving in thermodynamics, comprehension of and the ability to apply the principles of literary criticism, or translating English sentences into French. The test questions as a whole will be in sync with the objectives or aims of the course. As I indicated earlier, a valid test will assist in detecting student errors of both omission and commission so that appropriate help can be provided.

Formal studies are non-existent about the validity of classroom tests, that is, how many of them accurately reflect the aims or objectives of a course or course of study. But on the basis of certain lines of evidence, sound inferences can be made about their validity. The most important comes from a survey of a sample of around 40,000 faculty members (presumably representative of something over one-half million) conducted by the American Council on Education[5] a few years ago.

It was found that almost all of the respondents (some 97 percent) believed that the number one goal of undergraduate education was that of promoting among students the ability to engage in critical thinking or reasoning.

Yet as I document in Chapter 4, **Current College Tests,** the majority of test questions seek only information and isolated factual information at that. To spew information on a test or to recognize it as on a multiple-choice test is not to exhibit reasoning; note, too, that the few very abbreviated illustrations of course aims or objectives mentioned a couple of paragraphs earlier entail far more than mere information. Please! I am not even hinting that factual information is not important--it is just not enough!

Additional evidence about validity comes from the fact that many faculty members are not too clear in their own thinking about aims or objectives. An Associate Professor told me once that he would figure out the objectives after the course had ended. Patently, if the teacher's thinking is not too clear about aims, there is no way that test questions can be prepared which will measure them.

The final line of evidence comes from students. When given the opportunity, they (anonmously) make such comments about test validity in different courses as:

- Unrealistic questions -- trivial and not indicative of points that were stressed in the course.
- True-false and multiple-choice questions give a very poor indication of a student's knowledge.
- The tests were too picky.
- Questions often . . . not reflected as being significant information in lecture notes.
- The T/F questions made me feel we are being tested on the ability to take that kind of test.

All of these lines of evidence suggest that far too many classroom tests tend to be invalid; they do not examine for the attainment of common aims, such as reasoning, nor do they examine for the attainment of specific course aims.

When test results are dependable, the test is said to be reliable. We can "count on" the score of a given student being accurate. We want to count on a watch, a tire pressure guage, a fever thermometer, food scales, highway radar. Each of these testing devices, if poorly constructed or in the hands of an "untrained" user, is unreliable. On the other hand, if these instruments are constructed properly and used by a trained person, they are reliable and we can depend on the measurements.

All over the nation there are doubts about the reliability of highway radar--were we really going 62 as the device indicated? There have been countless court cases challenging radar accuracy (reliability).

Formal studies about the reliability of classroom tests are almost nonexistent; I was able to find two. The first one,[6] reported in 1954, surveyed faculties in 28 colleges and universities. Detailed data were not given, but it was concluded that little evidence was found of efforts being made by almost 1,000 college teachers to construct reliable tests for the measurement of learning their courses were supposed to promote.

In the other investigation,[7] almost 200 classroom tests were analyzed by sophisticated statistical procedures. The tests were from a great variety of courses--biology, economics, psychology, and others--at Pennsylvania State University. The reliabilities were found, on the average, to be very low; they ranged from those which were totally unreliable, as an elastic 6-foot tape measure would be--that is totally undependable, to a few which were very reliable.

There are at least four major sources of unreliability. The first is that of inadequate sampling of course content. A classroom test is always a sample of learning or achievement; thus a test should be a representative sample of the aims of the course. Generally speaking, the longer the test, the greater the chances of a representative sample and the greater the reliability.

The second source of unreliabilty is ambiguous questions. Each time an ambiguous question is read by a student, the meaning tends to be different; and certainly different students interpret ambiguous questions differently. This means we are not comparing students on the same instrument. The test results cannot be counted on. The English language is replete with words which are used ambiguously, and students read test questions more carefully than any other material they read.

Another source is negatively worded questions--they tend to confuse students. In the course of my inspections of tests, I found some with more than half the questions worded negatively. Try these two:

Which of the following is not true about both anthropology and psychology?
a) Anthropologists have questioned psychlogical generalizations based on the observation of individuals in Europe and the United States.
b) Anthropologists have helped to place the study of personality in the comparative perspective.
c) Anthropologists and other social scientists have demonstrated that average IQ differences between groups in a given society have environmental rather than genetic causes.
d) Anthropologists have done studies of personality in "primitive" societies.
e) All of the above are true.

Consequences of a physician contributing to substance abuse include all of the following, EXCEPT
a) drug dependence
b) organic brain syndrome
c) reinforcement of drug society
d) legal liability
e) all are possible consequences

I indicated the fourth source in the opening paragraphs of this chapter, essay questions tend to be unreliable--the causes are several: 1) a poorly worded or ambiguous question, 2) lack of clarity in the thinking of the grader, and 3) lack of agreement about the answers by two or more graders. But all of these deficiencies can be prevented or corrected.

Ponder this question for a few minutes and note how your notions about "the problems and its causes" shift and vacillate:

What is the urban transportation problem and what are its causes?

Ask the question of several friends! This is an ambiguous question--fine for provoking thoughtful discussions but not so for a test.

Unreliability is illustrated vividly by these words of students in different courses:

- Test was limited to very few things, even though it covered six chapters. There were only 20 questions (multiple choice) made up of insignificant information.
- The test questions were often irrelevant and ambiguous.
- Test questions tricky--need to be reworded. Some of the questions are absurb the way they are phrased. They can be interpreted too many ways.
- The fact that we only take two tests could place undue emphasis on a bad test.

Think about all the course tests you have taken. How many of them were valid and how many were reliable? The answers are few.

If you are sophisticated statistically, study the table in Appendix A and you can estimate the errors which were made in some of your grades. And what did those errors do to your GPA?

There are at least two additional aspects of quality--one of them is clarity of test directions and the other is the test format. An Astronomy test began with:

Read each question carefully. Indicate your choice for the correct answer by filling in the circle ( ) at the left of that answer. There are 22 questions listed, but you need answer only 20 questions. Each correct answer is worth 4 points.

One student answered all 22 and received a B. By answering the extra two correctly, there were enough points for an A. The professor wrote on the paper "I'm sorry, but to be fair I had to take the first 20 you answered."

How would you like to wade through four pages of this format from which these two questions came?

Which of the following best describes the long-run farm problem? (a) The demand for farm products has increased relative to their supply, but the highly elastic nature of agriculture demand has caused these shifts to result in declining farm incomes, (b) The supply of farm products has increased relative to the demand for them, and because demand is inelastic, farm prices and incomes have therefore declined, (c) The highly inelastic nature of agricultural demand has caused small year-to-year fluctuations in farm output to result in highly unstable farm incomes, (d) Lagging technology has decreased the productivity of farmers and therefore result in low farm prices and incomes.

Economic cost can best be defined as (a) all costs exclusive of payments to fixed factors of production, (b) compensations which must be received by resource owners to insure their continued supply, (c) any contractual obligation to labor or material suppliers, (d) any contractual obligation which results in a flow of money expenditures from an enterprise to resource suppliers.

Clinical Tests

Any serious discussion about tests and the nation's almost primitive worship of them must include some mention of medical laboratory ones. The costs, as in educational ones, may be human as well as monetary. Citizens need to learn to ask the right questions about these tests, too.

We hear and read of medical tests almost daily. A friend remarks: "I had these peculiar pains; I spent two days in the hospital undergoing tests. The bill was $1200." There are frequent news stories about doctors who order more tests than necessary because of fear of malpractice suits.

You read accounts such as this:

Dear Abby:[8] About the woman whose blood test came back positive and she swore there had to be a mistake: Fifteen years ago my son, who was to be married in two weeks, took a blood test and was informed that he had syphilis!
    His fiancee's father gave me the news and told me what a rotten son I had. He asked what they were going to do about the $5000 deposit they had paid the caterer, etc.
    My son took more blood tests, and finally the New York State Health Department advised us that some other factor in his blood caused the false positive. Wouldn't you think most doctors would be familiar with this? Well, they weren't.
                            F in NYC

According to physicians I consulted, numerous factors including certain prior diseases can cause false positives.

The Center for Disease Control in Atlanta estimated that clinical laboratories performed six billion tests in 1980. If the cost, let's be very very conservative so as not to put some of the great washed on the defensive, was $5 per test the total expenditure was $30,000,000,000. The six billion estimate may be too low. The lone hospital in a small town reported almost 300,000 tests in 1980, while one of several hospitals in a large city reported having conducted four and one-half million clinical laboratory tests in that year.

The issue of reliability is as applicable to clinical laboratory tests as it is to college classroom ones (and highway radar). Are they accurate? Can the results be counted on? If a test is repeated will the findings be essentially the same?

Two sets of factors, either separately or together, determine reliability: 1) the care with which a body specimen is obtained, i.e., a clean syringe being used for drawing blood, and 2) the care with which directions for analysis are followed.

As for validity--the extent to which a test measures what it is supposed to measure--two sets of factors either separately or together contribute to it: 1) the actual mechanics of the test, and 2) interpretations of the results. I used the syphilis illustration because it is an attention getter--imagine yourself in that predicament--and because both sets of factors went awry.

False labels do occur because of deficiencies in test mechanics, but most importantly, they result from incorrect interpretations of findings. These misinterpretations are made by people--medical specialists. Just as significant decisions are made about students by slavish devotion to numbers and the myth of objectivity so decisions are made about illness and health by unquestioning worship of some test number from a laboratory.

All numbers must be interpreted. Interpretations, decisions, and judgments are made by people. Some medical specialists, who ought to know better, are tyrannized by tests and, in turn, tyrannize their patients.

Two physicians, writing in the very prestigious New England Journal of Medicine[9] declare:

> In an era when the more expensive and the more technologic are equated with the better, the simple and the traditional are ignored. . .detailed histories and complete physical examinations. Computers and space-age technology should confirm and refine clinical impressions, not vice versa.

This explanation for excessive testing is offered in MEDICAL CHOICES, MEDICAL CHANCES:[10]

> ....Technical procedures, valuable as they are when there is a rational basis for using them, are invoked mindlessly and automatically, as rituals to reassure anxious physicians. Precise laboratory measurement is accepted as a substitute for a complex, elusive reality that may be understood only with patience and sensitivity....

But to return to the primary target of this book, college classroom tests, their influence on learning will be examined in the next chapter.

3

Influencing Learning

In how many of your college courses have you asked "Is that going to be on the final?" In how many of them did you also ask something to the effect "Will the test be objective or essay?" These two questions are without doubt the most frequently asked ones on any campus. The fact that they are raised repetitively from year to year and from course to course indicates widespread awareness among students that tests do indeed influence their learning.

I have inquired of audiences at many colleges and universities--audiences composed mostly of faculty members, with a few deans and an occasional chancellor or president--if they have heard these queries. Routinely at least three-fourths of the auditors, by a simple show of hands, responded "Yes." What has surprised me were the murmurs of astonishment at the results of the little poll. Members of the audiences must have been surprised, too, that their colleagues had heard the questions in their classes. But where have their minds been when the questions were directed to them? Engrossed solely in covering the material and explaining the textbook!!?

Some of the startled ones have been experimental scientists of various persuasions who are experts in measurement and thus well-versed in all the vicissitudes of it. One of these vicissitudes is the operation of the long-recognized Heisenberg Uncertainty Principle, also called the Principle of Indeterminancy, which states that the act of measurement influences the phenomenon(a) being measured. For example, a cold thermometer placed in a cup of hot tea will lower the temperature of the tea; there is an effect on the liquid, even though slight. And at least two factors or forces distort a true blood pressure reading: 1) the pressure of the inflated cuff and 2) for some people the very thought of the procedure.

Following one of my talks in which I had mentioned the Principle and suggested its operation in educational measurements, a professor of nuclear physics (a real expert about the Principle) approached with a look of bewilderment on his face and said, "Now, why hadn't I seen those connections?" I have been struck on many occasions by the apparent inability--or unwillingness--of faculty to apply knowledge from their fields of specialization to teaching-learning activities.

If you answered the two questions in the affirmative, you are well on your way to knowing the ways in which tests do indeed influence student achievement. If a teacher replies to the first query, "No, that will not be on the test," the fate is sealed of whatever gem it is--it is gone from the psychic repertoires of students. An indisputable influence! And knowledge of the type of test, objective or essay, will determine how much energy students will expend, how they go about studying, and what they learn. Anecdotal evidence abounds--for those who will look and listen--to support the notion that classroom tests influence learning.

What is so interesting here is that faculty members seem so unaware of this powerful teaching-learning tool, so unaware of the significance of these student inquiries, and so oblivious to the connection between their test concerns when they were students and those of their students now. One explanation is that many of them resent the time needed for class tests; most of us like to talk so much that anything which interferes is resented and resisted. Many faculty truly believe, too, that their talking really "learns" students.

A college president chided me once before an audience of his colleagues along the lines that this student anecdotal evidence just wasn't impressive and did not persuade him about the importance of classroom tests. To be convinced he wanted research results--numbers, if you will!

Of course, to be consistent with my position in earlier pages, faculties have been so caught up in serving as personnel-selection agents for society that all else about teaching-learning has paled. Perhaps a brief description of some of the research studies about the influence of tests on learning and a presentation of research evidence might be convincing to at least some of the skeptics. Tests are major teaching-learning devices at our disposal; with many students we need all the devices we can find.

Research studies about the influences of tests began to appear in the literature in the early 1930s. The first clear unequivocal statement I found appeared in 1934:[1] "The kind of test to be given, if the students know it in advance, determines in large measure both what and how they study." This conclusion emerged from an investigation at the University of Alabama with 135 students in psychology classes. The students had been provided a check list of study methods and asked to indicate which ones they used in preparation for different types of tests--those requiring mere recognition of a correct answer (multiple-choice and true-false) versus requiring recall or remembering of content (completion and essay).

At about the same time, a similar study was conducted at the University of Minnesota.[2] Students reported that they studied differently for different type tests; for recognition ones they focused upon details and exact wording, while for recall tests they tried to perceive relationships and trends.

I'll describe some studies in detail. Skip to the conclusions if you like, but the details are here because around 99 percent of faculty members do not read either the past or the current literature from which these investigations have been drawn. Further studies would be useful, and some faculty might be provoked by these--or you might raise questions with faculty which will challenge them.

Two studies at the University of Michigan[3] in 1935 provided considerable clarification of the Alabama general conclusion. In the first one, four groups of students were asked to study two mimeographed chapters of material unfamiliar to them about the Civil War. Each group was instructed to prepare to take <u>one</u> of these type tests: true-false, multiple-choice, completion, or essay. In fact, immediately following three two-hour supervised study periods, all students took all four of the tests. Five weeks later the tests were repeated.

Students who had studied under the impression they would take either completion or essay performed better on all the tests than did students who were studying for the true-false or multiple-choice ones. This was true for both the immediate and delayed (five weeks later) tests. Of further enduring interest are the findings about how the students studied. They were asked, "Tell how you studied for your particular type of examination," and "Did you study differently for this type of examination?" At the same time, the researchers perused the notes they had made and the study booklets, which they had been free to mark.

As for the two questions, the remarks of one of the students summarize the essence of what most of them said:

> . . . . When studying for completion, multiple-choice or true-false examinations, I find that I do not attempt to get a general view of the material--I try to learn the facts or memorize the statements. When I study for an essay examination, I read and re-read the material with the object of getting not only the facts but also a general concept of the material.

Remember this was a college student speaking around 1934--even before I entered college.

As I read that statement in 1980, or almost half a century later, it sounded so familiar I thought I'd better investigate further. I asked several of my colleagues in different fields to ask a few students--any they wished to choose--these two questions: 1) How do you go about studying for an objective test? and 2) How do you go about studying for an essay test? You guessed it--it was hard to tell the difference between the answers of almost 50 years ago and those of today. One student reflected the views of most:

When studying for an objective test, certain facts have to be memorized—names, dates, places, etc. are a must to know. I find it easier to just read my notes over and over; and if there are lists of some sort, I may just write them over and over until I have memorized them. A lot of times memorization is not essential; just being able to recognize an answer is enough.

When studying for an essay test, memorization is not that helpful and at times impossible. Usually the material covered in an essay test is a great amount. I just try to understand the material as best I can and try to know the most important points that were brought across in class. Then I make sure I understand how all the material is related and how it pertains to the class.

Progress!! "In the year of our Lord 1432, there arose a grievous quarrel among the brethren over the number of teeth in the mouth of a horse...."

Analysis of the Michigan students' study notes and of the study booklets revealed that six study methods were used: 1) the underlining of words, phrases, and sentences in the booklet; 2) the listing of names, places, dates, and numbers; 3) the taking of random notes; 4) the making of summaries in paragraph form; 5) the drawing of maps; and 6) the framing of practice test questions. The most noteworthy results were that a smaller percentage of students in the essay group used underlining, and a greater percentage of them made summaries and maps than did those in any of the other three groups.

The second Michigan study was conducted as part of regular classwork so as to be more for real than are laboratory learning studies. An entire chapter on Memory from the textbook formed the basis of the learning material. The procedure was like that of the first study but had three added features: students had an extra study period, heard the material discussed in class, and received these sample test questions as part of the initial instructions:

<u>Essay</u> -- Discuss as fully as possible the three methods which have been used in studying rote memory. What does each of these methods measure?
<u>True-False</u> -- Ebbinghaus used the prompting method in his studies of rote memory.
<u>Completion</u> -- The "savings method" measures _____.
<u>Multiple-Choice</u> -- Ebbinghaus used the (savings, prompting, paired associates) method in his studies of rote memory.

(Compare these old questions with the current ones I've scattered through the book. Not many differences!? "For 13 days the disputation raged without ceasing....")

The essay group (the one studying for that type test) performed better on all the tests, both immediate and delayed (four weeks later), than did the other three groups. The completion group was superior to the true-false and multiple-choice ones.

A study[4] very similar to these was conducted in England in 1970 but with quite different learning material. Sixty students were divided into four groups of fifteen each, and all studied a paper about the genetic code. Those who studied under the impression they would be required to produce a summary of the paper outperformed (on all tests) those who were preparing for a multiple-choice or a completion test, both immediately and one week following the original study session.

At least one clear conclusion emerges (and is supported by other studies); students who prepare to take essay tests outperform students who prepare to take other type tests. Of major importance is the fact that the superiority lasts over a period of time. The Michigan and England studies are unusual in that almost all studies of improving college classroom learning confine concern to end-of-course performance. It goes without saying that most courses aim toward more enduring learning.

I believe the explanation for the essay superiority is fairly simple and fits with the everyday learning experiences of most of us. After all, we have been learning since we were born. Most of us know that it is easier to recognize a date or name, for example, than it is to recall one. That is, we can know something less well for recognition purposes than for recollection ones. Most classroom multiple-choice and true-false tests require students only to recognize an answer.

Quality essay tests require a great deal more than mere recollection, but students know that being able to recall or remember is a prominent feature in them. As a consequence they study harder when anticipating an essay test.

Now I do not mean to imply that recognition and recall are the whole story. Far from it! But these two mental activites seem to be essential to the entire learning endeavor and to utilizing higher order mental processes.

When used to indicate that something has been learned by a college learner, the term "learning" includes a multitude of mental and emotional phenomena--the acquisition of simple facts, a grasp of concepts and ideas, changes in reasoning patterns, shifts in a galaxy of complex attitudes and values, alterations in interests, and others. Memorizing historical dates surely requires different intellectual and affective exercising than does developing the ability to weigh ideas.

It is for these reasons that learning classification schemes have been devised. I mention these overly simplified descriptions to emphasize the undue simplicity of many, many classroom tests and because these terms will be popping up throughout the book. The major elements of most of the schemes include Information, Comprehension, Application, and Evaluation. Moreover, these seem to be the basic mental features most of us wish to see developed in college students; these are the ones used by most of us in our everyday callings.

<u>Information</u> -- the possession of material learned previously; it varies from isolated facts to complicated concepts. Information is either recognized or recalled. Memorizing is useful in acquiring some information. This reflects the lowest level of learning.

<u>Comprehension</u> -- a synonym here is understanding of content or material. It is manifested by putting something into one's own words, by explaining something to others, or by summarizing something into a few words.

<u>Application</u> -- as the term implies, this means using what one has learned, for example, arithmetic symbols and manipulations in problem solving.

<u>Evaluation</u> -- this is the highest level of learning and includes critical thinking or reasoning, judging the value of material, deciding about significance, and so on.

Unfortunately, the influence of tests upon the higher-order mental processes has not been studied very extensively. I am willing, though, to generalize--until proven otherwise--that there is applicability. I am also willing to generalize the findings from this very carefully conducted study[5] in eighth grade history to college classrooms.

Quizzes were given every week for eight weeks. For half the students, the quizzes required recall of facts from the text; for the other half, the quizzes required the drawing of inferences about the effects of selected events on different economic, religious, or geographic interest groups. At the end of eight weeks, all students took three tests: recall of facts, drawing <u>new</u> inferences, and drawing inferences from unrelated material.

Both groups performed similarly on the fact test; the inference group did significantly better in drawing new inferences about special interest groups in United States history; there were no differences in inference scores on the unrelated material. Remember, these were 14-year-olds. It would be my guess that college students having been tested for a term on drawing inferences would do better also on drawing them from unrelated materials.

A current teaching arrangement[6] in a genetics course is revealing that frequent problem-solving questions with immediate feedback via the computer results in better performance with problem-type questions on the final exam. The influence of problem solving questions on later critical thinking or reasoning needs to be studied much more extensively.

Another test factor influencing learning is the frequency of testing. And while the results are by no means clear-cut, the generalization seems warranted that frequent testing (within limits) during a term results in higher performance on a final exam. The catch is "how frequent." The answer seems to be more frequent than a mid-term and a final. How's that for academic hedging?

A recent study[7] utilized weekly tests. The study was unusual in that the goals of the course were reported, and the central focus was on process rather than on content. For example, students were required to evaluate critically the current methods by which psychologists go about confronting and investigating major concerns. Very serious efforts were made to prepare test items that measured something other than knowledge of facts:

> According to the frustration-aggression model, the more children are punished, the more strongly they will want to misbehave (i.e., the more frustration, the more they will be aggressive). Some parents of children are interviewed with a tape recorder, and each family is given a punishing score. The teachers of the children write short essays describing each child, and each child is given a misbehavior score. Suppose that there is a significant trend ($r = .54$ $p < .01$) for children with high misbehavior scores to have parents with high punishing scores. From this one study, we can conclude that: a) the model is proved, b) the model is disproved, c) the model is supported and fits the available data, d) none of the above.

(Classroom multiple-choice questions of this quality are rare, but did you catch the sentence structure errors and the test error?)

Students who took tests each week of the term outperformed those who had a mid-term and a final. Perhaps the explanation for frequent tests enhancing learning is simple. Many students need to be forced to study; tests serve that purpose. Other students are incapable of managing their time; tests sort of put them on a schedule.

The complexities of teaching-learning which many of us often ignore in our dash for facile panaceas are illustrated by one investigation in which it was found that difficult multiple-choice tests facilitated learning for average and above average college students to a greater extent than did easy exams.[8] This seems quite consistent to me with the essay test findings from the Michigan and England studies.

As we draw this chapter to a close, it is well to remember that many students study solely to make grades. Since this is the case, let's improve the tests upon which the grades are based. In that way we will increase the odds of improving all facets of learning.

Have you ever wondered why girls tend to do better academically than boys? One of the reasons for this is that the girls know how to study. Note the wisdom of one coed.[9]

> The recipe for success at a large university goes something like this: Start the semester by getting a boyfriend. In the first weeks of the semester, devote all your time to him. There is no point at all in studying during the first weeks of class. Pay little attention to what the professor says about grading, for his information is generally vague and misleading. Pay a little more attention to what the teaching assistant says, but don't consider his information to be too reliable. When it comes time for the first test, skim over your notes and the assigned reading material, but don't read it carefully. There is little point in making a concerted effort at this time because you don't know the system of testing and grading that is going to be used and there is no point to study until you understand how you will be tested.
> After you get back your first test, study the test. Try to figure out on the basis of the questions and the method of scoring what is going to be asked in the future and how it should be answered.
> After you develop your theory of tests and grading, begin to taper off with the boyfriend and devote some time to reading and planning for taking the next test. In the last few days before the test, devote some intensive work to preparing for the test that you think will be given.
> When you get back your second test, you evaluate your theory regarding testing and grading. If you really did well, then you continue your preparation procedures and, towards the end of the semester, you drop your boyfriend and devote all your attention to preparing for the test that you now feel confident will be given.
> If you did not do as well as you expected, drop your boyfriend and examine the tests again until you have a better perception of what sort of test is being written.

The secret of success is simply to learn how to take tests that are given. In order to do this, one must examine the tests that actually are given. The objectives instructors may talk about are usually quite irrelevant to the way they test and grade. Most talk should be ignored. After all, grades are what count, and you get good grades by doing well on tests.

Finally, there was the professor of Religious Studies who term after term gave only one test and always asked the same lone question: "Discuss the troubles of Moses and the Children of Israel as they wandered in the wilderness."

One day his dean garnered the courage--he did not wish to be accused of violating academic freedom--to suggest to him that he cease asking the same question repeatedly because surely the students were studying nothing else. Without informing his charges of the change-to-be, at the next final exam, this question was written on the board: "Criticize the Sermon on the Mount."

The students were stunned, they were bewildered. Some were ashen as they left the room, having handed in blank papers. One young fellow remained; he wrote and wrote and wrote. The Prof could hardly wait to see the results of his efforts--this is what he read: "Far be it from me to criticize the Sermon on the Mount, but let me tell you what I know about Moses and the Children of Isreal. . . ."

4

Current College Tests

Faculty members in concert with members of other organizations and professions are loathe to scrutinize their own fiefdoms. What sets us--faculties--apart, though, from members of the other great washed guilds is our insistence upon the absolute necessity for free and untrammelled inquiry into all features of life.

Despite this caveat, there are severe limitations to any full discovery of the quality of current classroom tests in the 3,000-odd colleges and universities inhabited by over one-half million faculty members. These limitations exist because we have examined and scrutinized others to a far greater extent than we have examined and scrutinized ourselves.

Fortunately there are occasional heretics who do investigate from within. And as I have indicated already, I believe that the limited findings paraded herein from a few colleges and universities are representative of the majority. After all most faculty members come from a small number of graduate schools and have been indoctrinated (albeit indirectly) about teaching in comparable ways. Would that someone will try to prove my generalizations about inferior tests to be grossly incorrect!

By calculated design and with specific intent, I open this chapter with reference to the University of California, Berkeley--identified mostly in academic circles as just plain Berkeley. There is a decided pecking order among colleges and universities, and Berkeley is at or near the top in the thinking of many; it is surely within the top 10. Notice I am not putting it number 1--I am not that temerous and since I was never a student there, it cannot be!

The exalted ranking means that all the lesser schools, except others of the top 10, try to copy Berkeley because its practices are beyond reproach and therefore to be emulated. (Berkeley and others of the top 10, by the way, attract huge numbers of federal dollars or they did at one time!) If I can demonstrate--and I can--that classroom tests at Berkeley are of poor quality, then some other schools might be less defensive and more willing to examine their tests.

The Free Speech Movement of '64 (the campus disturbances that were the initial sparks for student protests all over) was so pervasively disruptive at Berkeley as to move the faculty to undertake a rather thorough study of undergraduate education there.[1] Among other investigative procedures, questionnaires were distributed to a random sample of almost 2,600 students in the fall of 1965. Over 2,000 students replied; this is a remarkably high return.

The major question of interest to us here was "How well do you think the grading system at Berkeley reflects the student's actual knowledge and understanding of the subjects studied?" This was the only question about tests and/or grades and perhaps reveals the small degree of importance attached to tests and grades by the faculty--a minimal interest seems to be true elsewhere, too.

I'm sure you recognize the question is one of very poor quality. It is ambiguous--the term "grading system" means different things to different people. As used by some, it refers to single questions on tests; to others it refers to the assigning of the symbols ABCDF; and to others it encompasses the entire process from the quality and types of individual questions to the letter symbol being recorded on the transcript. Here it must refer to the entire process. Furthermore, there is no single grading standard on that campus or any other large one; there are grading standards--the assigning of the symbols--such as those mentioned in the first chapter.

At any rate, slightly over half the students (53 percent) responded either "very well" or "fairly well." The remaining 47 percent indicated that the grading system reflected a student's actual knowledge and understanding "only slightly" or "not at all"; they were very critical. The authors of the final report were careful to emphasize that enthusiastic support should not be expected for any form of grading system, but that it is time to pay attention when two-fifths or 40 percent of over 800 honor students (in a separate analysis) express considerable dissatisfaction. As I recall, standards were much higher then (some 15 years ago) than now for honors work.

On the basis of my experience with thousands of students, I would say that the negative reactions were mainly to individual classroom tests. The students probably reacted directly to invalidity and unreliability in the same fashion as did those students quoted in Chapter 2. In this connection, of special pertinence was the large number of students who chose to write in criticisms of the excessive reliance on objective questions and the fact that memorization of isolated information was the key to doing well on them.

Although a systematic study of the faculty about tests was not undertaken, several of them volunteered comments. One professor wrote:

> I have found that I cannot mark with any pretense of fairness several hundred essays. . . . I have, therefore, taken to objective examinations demanding factual answers, which I dislike extremely but consider less unfair than badly marked essays. I think it is ridiculous that a physicist or engineer should find his career depending on whether he gets a "B" or "C" in my course. . . .

Another professor wrote:

> I have very little confidence in the grades turned in as a result of examinations read by twenty different teaching assistants, many of them grading for the first time, in a class of a thousand. Almost without regard to the seriousness of the effort by the faculty, such numbers put a premium on the easiest and most efficient methods of grading, rather than on the most serious ones.

The utterance "I have very little confidence in the grades turned in by twenty different teaching assistants. . . ." is one very worthy of elaboration. It was found during the investigation that almost one-third of all the classes taken by the graduating class of 1965 had been taught regularly by Graduate Teaching Assistants. GTA's are the people whose major purpose for being on campus is for the pursuit of advanced degrees. For many of them, the teaching is incidental and most of them receive no supervision.

At the time of the study, a little over 40 percent of freshmen and sophomore classes had been taught by Graduate Teaching Assistants. While it is impossible to say how many of these novices prepared and corrected tests, I am confident a considerable number did so. I am equally confident that their products were of poor quality.

I say this because the basic requisite for preparing test questions is a thorough mastery of subject matter; this means at the least being acquainted with facts and principles, attuned to their implications, and aware of popular fallacies and misconceptions. Most Graduate Teaching Assistants do not have such mastery—why should they be expected to? Additional requisites are an ability to write with clarity and the time required to do so. Berkeley is not alone, by any means, in using large numbers of Teaching Assistants for undergraduate instruction.

I doubt very much if there have been substantive improvements at Berkeley over the intervening 15 years; the markedly increased enrollments since 1965 and the academic grapevine suggest there has not. I suspect there has been further erosion.

I am really in conflict about presenting the tables of percentages in the next few pages. On the one hand, these are boring to many people and thus are to be avoided in this type book. On the other, I believe they will help in conveying my notions clearly. The very word "tests" tends to arouse strong feelings in most of us, so much so that extra caution is useful in discussions about them. Reason sometimes slips at their mention. This is one instance in which numbers serve as good evidence.

One of the first fairly extensive investigations about classroom tests was conducted at the University of Illinois only a decade ago.[2] Questionnaires seeking information about testing practices in undergraduate courses were mailed to slightly over 5,000 faculty members. Only 1,700 were returned; this low sort of return is to be expected from faculty on most campuses. It is my impression that it is the interested faculty who cooperate--thus the true picture is worse than the one presented.

This table indicates the frequencies with which various test types were used. Be wary, now, of the numbers--the numbers do not tell the whole story. Note, too, I am not using the collective and obfuscating terms "objective" and "subjective."

Recognition Tests		Recall Plus Tests	
Multiple-choice	14%	Essay	17%
True-false	9	Short-Answer Essay	24
Matching	7	Fill-in-blank	12

Remember I suggested in Chapter 3 that certain type tests required only the mental process of recognizing while other types required recalling, still others applying, and so on. I used the heading, "Recall Plus Tests" in the table because good quality essay questions require much, much more than mere recall or recollection.

If we combine multiple-choice, true-false, and matching types, then almost one-third of the questions required only recognition--the lowest form of learning--and more than likely just recognition of isolated factual information.

Note the profundity of these three recognition questions:

The Philippine Insurrection broke out in February:
  a. 1898
  b. 1899
  c. 1900
  d. 1902

Tradition has it that the Compromise of 1877 was worked out:
a. by President Ulysses S. Grant
b. between Hayes and Tilden
<u>c.</u> at the Wormley Hotel
<u>d.</u> both a and c

The national rate of illiteracy in 1900 was:*
a. 2%
<u>b.</u> 10.7%
c. 20%
d. 40.5%

The letter preceding each correct alternative has been underlined so that you may consider yourself further enlightened. Did you know about the Wormley Hotel? The "illiteracy" question probably promotes reverence for numbers and facilitates being numbed by them. The measurement of the extent of illiteracy in 1900 was not at all as accurate as the correct answer implies--nor are the measurements of that problem and others such as the level of unemployment and the Gross National Product accurate to tenths of points even today!

If we combine the fill-in-blank types with the short answer essay ones in the table--I'm suspicious of this last type in that I'll bet only two or three words were required for an answer--then slightly over one-third of the items required only <u>recall</u> of nothing more than factual information.

Two-thirds of the questions are now accounted for; only the two lowest levels of learning were required. As shown in the table, 17 percent of the questions were essay ones, but we should not be misled by the implications of the term "essay." What we would like to think about the quality of these essay questions may not be the case. Read on.

Faculty respondents had been asked to weigh four factors commonly considered when scoring essay questions--organization, style, knowledge of facts, and originality. Then rank orders of the importance of the four factors were determined for each academic department. Sixty-nine percent of the departments ranked the factors--most to least important--knowledge of facts, originality, organization, and style. Knowledge of facts was most important in all but two departments.

I infer, then, that the bulk of the essay questions also got at isolated factual information. As you may recall, I insisted in Chapter 2 that whether a test was objective or subjective, multiple-choice or essay, was <u>not</u> the fundamental issue. The issue is that of the substance of a question--information, comprehension, evaluation, and so on.

---

*Publisher Permissions for these three questions accompanying textbooks will be found in the Notes and Acknowledgments section.

A mere 13 percent of the test questions were of the problem solving type (3 percent were classified as "other" in the formal report).

To change the pace, read this passage from a play and note the questions asked about it in a drama course.

> . . . and there he is now, with his great confiding child-like mind, compassed about with all this treachery—living under the same roof with such a creature, and never dreaming that what he calls his home is built upon a lie. (<u>Comes a step nearer</u>) When I look back upon your past, I seem to see a battle-field with shattered lives on every hand.
>
> _____ says this to _____ in the play, _____, by _____.

Just what is the point of a question of this type?

Another line of evidence to support my assertion about the factual nature of the test questions comes from the Illinois students who were surveyed as part of the same study. Eighty-two percent of almost 3,500 students agreed with this statement in a questionnaire:

> Despite instructors' insistence that they do not teach facts, most grades are based on tests which are primarily factual in content.

(Eighty-seven percent of approximately 400 graduating seniors at the University of Tennessee agreed with the statement. Yes, this item deserves criticism, too.)

Further enlightenment is added by knowing something about the composition of the group of 3,500 Illinois students. When the results were analyzed by class level—freshman, sophomore, junior, and senior—there were essentially no differences among the percentages of agreement with the statement; approximately 80 percent in each class agreed. Surely we ought to require higher order mental activities from juniors and seniors than from freshmen and sophomores.

Four-fifths of the students from the College of Liberal Arts and Sciences of the University of Illinois agreed with the statement! Yet almost all catalogs are fond of proclaiming something to the effect: The liberal arts education provides the individual with the ability to comprehend the great outlines of knowledge, the principles upon which it rests, the scale of its parts, its lights and shadows. A liberally educated person is identified by quality of mind.

The attainment of these saintly qualitites can be assisted and then whether they are possessed can be determined by carelessly prepared true-false, multiple-choice, or fill-in-blank questions!!!? Wow!! The catalog implication is, of course, that professional programs (e.g., engineering) do not produce such wonders.

In another survey of a different group of Illinois students, almost 90 percent of 500 agreed with this statement: "Most objective examinations call for factual information." I am familiar with the faculty denials! "Those things don't happen in my department and my tests are really good" or "We just have too many students."

It is so easy to dismiss the problem of poor tests in this manner, but maybe these sorts of denials and large enrollments are not the explanations. There could be some hidden or not so obvious pervasive factors at work. The next table contains the results of a similar survey in two highly regarded very small midwest liberal arts colleges[3] (the Illinois percentages are in parentheses):

Recognition Tests		Recall Plus Tests	
Multiple Choice	17% (14)	Essay	13% (17)
True-false	13 (9)	Short answer essay	16 (24)
Matching	9 (7)	Fill-in blanks	10 (12)

Note the remarkably similar usages of test types in a huge institution and in two very small ones. If anything the picture is a bit worse in the latter because their claims for the saintly attainments of their students often exceed those made by the giants. I'll parade some more evidence and then I'll talk about the pervasive factors.

In late 1978 questionnaires were sent to all or almost all 500 faculty members at The University of Tennessee, Knoxville who were teaching introductory courses;[4] approximately 150 completed forms were returned. As I indicated for the Illinois study, this is a poor return rate--a little less than one-third. Again I believe it is the interested faculty who cooperate in these endeavors; the true picture may be worse than the one presented.

The table indicates the frequencies with which various test types were used in the introductory courses.

Recognition Tests		Recall Plus Tests	
Multiple-choice	17%	Essay	10%
True-false	13	Short answer essay	16
Matching	7	Fill-in-blank	13

Slightly over one-third of the test items are of the recognition type or the lowest level of learning variety. When these are combined with the Fill-in-Blank types, over half of the tests call for factual information.

In a general way, there are remarkable similarities in the percentages for the usage of specific test types among the four schools--Illinois, two small schools, and Tennessee. For example, recognition items constitute 30 percent, 39 percent, and 37 percent respectively in those institutions. The fact that the Illinois study was conducted approximately 10 years before the others may explain the smaller percentage there; I suspect it is larger now.

Problem solving items contributed 16 percent and "other" was 9 percent at Tennessee. The Tennessee faculty was asked also "Which item types do you find most difficult to write?" Multiple-choice and True-false ones were clearly the winners. I hope all faculty realize that this is the case.

Five Nebraska schools were studied recently[5]--Union College, Chadron and Kearney State Colleges, and the University of Nebraska at Omaha and at Lincoln. These institutions represent a small private college, two medium-sized ones, and two state universities of large enrollments. Approximately half of the faculties in each school participated.

Separate statistics are not given for each school because there were no important differences among them in test type frequencies. This means that the frequencies of usage for given test types were essentially the same at a small school with an enrollment of only 900 as at a large one with an enrollment of 22,000.

The questionnaire did not seek exactly the same information as had been sought from the schools already discussed in this chapter; hence this table is slightly different from the others. Faculties were asked to indicate on a five-point scale how often they typically used a specified test type. The table shows the percentages for "frequently" used combined with used "almost always."

Recognition Test		Recall Plus Tests	
Multiple Choice	37.5%	Essay	25.2%
		Short-Answer Essay	45.4
		Fill-in-blanks	16.1

(True-false and matching tests were not mentioned in the official report. The total is greater than 100 percent because a respondent could check more than one of the categories.)

Again we find remarkable similarities of usage in what adds up now to nine colleges and universities--recognition and recall, the lowest levels of learning, are those levels tested most often. I'm suspicious of the "Recall

Plus" percentages because in the same survey, nearly half (47 percent) of almost 4,500 students reported they had never or rarely written an essay exam. One of the difficulties in understanding findings of this sort is that the term "short essay" is interpreted idiosyncratically—it means different things to different faculty members.

In a study at the University of Washington[6] about the assigning of grades (ABCDF), 700 of nearly 2,200 faculty members were asked to divide 100 points among 12 factors which they used as their bases for grades in one of their classes. The question to them was "Indicate how much importance you attach to each of the following sources of information in assigning grades by dividing 100 points among those you use for this class." More ambiguity, I might add.

Objective exams—not described further but usually multiple-choice, true-false, and matching—received 37 points on the average and essay exams received 17 on the average. These weights seem quite consistent with the percentages of usage in the several other schools already mentioned.

Physics departments in England and Wales[7] were queried about examinations; student test papers from 12 of them were analyzed. Each question was categorized according to one of the three following schemes:

i) Memory: the whole question could be answered by direct recall of material likely to be dealt with in a lecture course and certainly available in standard textbooks.
ii) Mixed: part of the question of type (i) and part of type (iii).
iii) Application: the whole of the question demanded either the application of standard material to a particular problem, or the reorganization and correlation of routine or textbook material for a particular purpose.

It was found that almost half of the questions were type i (Memory) and only 15 percent were type iii (Applications); the remainder were type ii or mixed. Final year papers were analyzed from another ten schools according to the same scheme. The results were almost identical.

In a similar investigation,[8] experts independently categorized hundreds of test items from such courses as physiology and chemistry. There was unanimous agreement among three judges that over half the questions demanded either recognition or recall of isolated information. Fewer than one-fourth of the questions were thought by any single judge to require even simple elements of interpretation of data or of problem solving.

In the study of reliability (mentioned in Chapter 2) at Pennsylvania State University of almost 200 classroom tests from a great variety of courses—biology, economics, psychology, and others—it was found that the questions were overwhelmingly of the factual type.[2]

A survey of tests used in medical schools[9] revealed that most exams in those institutions require recall of isolated facts or bits of information.

What all this evidence adds up to is the conclusion that most test questions for undergraduates and for some advanced students require a grasp of factual information and little more. There is almost no emphasis via test questions on the higher order mental processes of comprehending, applying, and evaluating. Size of the school does not seem to be the causative agent.

While I have paraded a few isolated test questions here and there, note this entire test. You do not have to be a physiologist to detect its limited nature:

Name (Print)_____ Section #_____

Matching 1-10
- (1) Androgens
- (2) Thyroxine
- (3) Growth Hormone
- (4) Estrogen
- (5) Insulin
- (6) All of the above
- (7) None of the above

____ 1. Stimulates protein synthesis
____ 2. Produced by the anterior pituitary
____ 3. Essential for glucose uptake by the brain
____ 4. Antagonistic to glucagon
____ 5. Produced by the islet cells of the pancreas
____ 6. Stimulates body growth
____ 7. Increases rate of osteoblast mitosis
____ 8. Synergistic with growth hormone
____ 9. Secreted by exocrine cells
____ 10. Cretinism results from deficiency of

True-False

____ 11. Chymotrypsin is secreted by the stomach.
____ 12. Gastrin inhibits HCl production.
____ 13. Most digestion and absorption takes place in the duodenum.
____ 14. Insulin deficiency causes a lowering of blood glucose.
____ 15. Growth hormone causes increased glycogen breakdown.
____ 16. Glucagon causes increased glucose uptake by muscle.
____ 17. Elevated epinephrine results in decreased gluconeogenesis.
____ 18. Insulin deficiency generally leads to hypertension.
____ 19. Decreased blood glucose stimulates insulin secretion.
____ 20. Acromegaly is a form of the "zits".
____ 21. Glycogen is found only in the liver.

____22. Epinephrine stimulates the formation off adipose-tissue TG deposition.
____23. Triglycerides are stored mainly in muscle.
____24. Microvilli are found in the luminal cells of the stomach.
____25. Bone growth is stimulated by somatomedin.

Matching 26-35
    (1) Trypsin   (5) Ribonuclease
    (2) Carboxypeptidase   (6) All of the above
    (3) Lipase   (7) None of the above
    (4) Amylase

____26. Produced by the pancreatic acinar cells
____27. Involved in the digestion of starch
____28. Produced in the stomach
____29. Also produced by the parotid gland
____30. Splits nucleic acids into free mononucleotids
____31. CCK stimulates the secretion of
____32. Emusifies fats
____33. Sight and smell of food stimulates secretion of
____34. Is relesed in the form of zymogen granules
____35. Is activated by HCl produced in the stomach

Matching 35-50
    (1) Gastrin   (6) 1, 2, and 3
    (2) Secretin   (7) 2 and 3
    (3) Cholecytorinin   (8) 4, 5
    (4) Insulin
    (5) Glucagon

____36. Inhibits gastric motility
____37. Stimulates gastric motility
____38. Mainly stimulates bicarbonate secretion
____39. Stimulates stomach secretion of HCl
____40. Inhibits gastric HCl secretion
____41. Produced by the pancreas
____42. Secreted by the duodenum
____43. Amino acids and fatty acids in the duodenum stimulates release of
____44. Are involved in the "absorptive state" of digestion and metabolism
____45. Are involved in the "postabsorptive state" of organic metabolism
____46. Stimulates gluconeogenesis
____47. Stimulates glycogenolysis
____48. Elevates plasma glucose
____49. Quantitatively more important in the contraction of the gallbladder

___50. Quantitatively more important in stimulation of pancreatic enzyme secretion

There are several quite plausible and pervasive explanations for faculty complacency: 1) the construction of quality tests is a difficult and time consuming task and the correcting of large numbers of papers can be very boring; 2) many faculty members and students really believe that even carelessly prepared multiple-choice and true-false questions are objective and therefore fair; 3) some faculty do not think testing is important and they resent class time being used for it; and 4) there is insufficient recognition that the measurement of human achievement is inordinately difficult--this is a polite way of saying ignorance abounds.

It is not restricted to faculties--a dean in a very well known and highly regarded university asserted: "Tests in any course make sense only in the context of the particular aims of the course and individual questions cannot be evaluated outside the context of the whole test." You have seen exceptions in this book already and you'll see many more; too bad this guy isn't right. What he's doing is rationalizing about the tests he gave when he was in the classroom. I'll bet he hasn't even seen any faculty tests since becoming dean. True or False--"Fiscal policy influences economic activity in the economy!"

Large classes, in my very considered opinion, are not the significant reason for poor quality tests.

I indicated earlier that faculty members, generally, do not receive training in their craft. In the Tennessee study, they were asked how they learned about test construction. Almost three-fourths stated "on my own"--meaning no formal instruction. But what gave me significant pause was the fact that slightly over one-fourth attributed their skills to intuition. Poor students!! What is the meaning of a GPA?

Supporting evidence comes from the study of marketing courses which we will discuss in the next chapter; 82 percent of these faculty members attributed their test-construction skills to learning by trial and error.

Excellent, and some inexpensive, books* are readily available (most of them are in college and university libraries) which can be useful in depriving faculties of this self-imposed ignorance. ". . . he beseeched them to unbend in a manner coarse and unheard of, and to look in the open mouth of a horse. . . ."

---

*See Appendix B

5

Other Test Frailties

I mentioned in the all too condensed testing history in Chapter 2 that during the late 1950's publishers began to provide test questions to faculties for use with their textbooks. By now the supplying of these questions is big business; the practice has become more or less routine for many publishers and many textbooks. (This is one of the factors contributing to increased textbook costs--these are, of course, passed on to students). The questions come to the faculty as part of an instructor's manual; some faculty demand also that the questions be supplied via computer tapes.

The availability of the questions is a major inducement for a faculty member to adopt a particular textbook. Contrary to the public schools where most individual teachers have little to do with final decisions about the texts they will use, most college and university faculty members have the sole say about books for their courses.

Publishers of different texts for the same course, for example, Introductory Psychology, are more or less forced to supply test items to meet the competition--faculty fringe benefits. There is no way of determining with any degree of preciseness the extent to which such questions are used in college classrooms, but the fact they accompany so many textbooks suggests they are used on a grand scale--by hundreds of thousands.

Presently textbook publisher questions are provided for introductory courses in accounting, American history, biology, chemistry, computer science, economics, education, English, geography, geology, management, marketing, mathematics, physics, political science, psychology, sociology, statistics, western civilization, zoology, and others. Questions are provided, too, for an occasional advanced course. The majority of all the questions are multiple-choice and true-false.

But the important issue is: What is the quality of these publisher questions? I was able to find only three formal studies of them. In the first[1], questionnaires had been analyzed from 173 faculty members who taught courses in marketing and who represented colleges and universities in 43 states and the District of Columbia. (This was a questionnaire return rate of slightly less than one of two.) Close to 80 percent of these faculty use multiple-choice questions to some extent and 20 percent use them exclusively.

A decided majority of the respondents indicated that half or more of the publisher supplied multiple-choice questions were unsatisfactory in one way or another. According to these faculty, their inadequacies included: 1) focusing on trivia, 2) some part of the item being stated ambiguously or phrased awkwardly, 3) two or more alternatives being correct, and 4) no answer being correct. Over half agreed with this statement: "The majority of multiple-choice questions in instructor's manuals focus on rote memorization" (still another bad item).

Here, of course, is additional evidence for the conclusion reached in Chapter 4 about the majority of college questions. The lowest level of learning, recognition, is that level tested most often. This means that these tests tend to be invalid because you can be sure that marketing faculties claim the development in students of such qualities as applying and evaluating. The excessive inadequacies, especially the ambiguities and awkward phrases, mean that the tests are unreliable; one cannot count on the results.

So to the question, "What is the quality of these publisher marketing questions?", the answer is "Poor."

At the same time, less than one in five of these faculty respondents believed it was imperative that publisher supplied textbook questions be improved. And consistently a majority indicated that the quality of the supplied items was of no importance in adopting a textbook. Apparently these faculty aren't too concerned about the quality of their tests even though they criticized the publishers.

I am willing to generalize once more and suggest that similar deficiencies exist on a comparable scale for publisher questions in many other fields and that faculties therein hold attitudes comparable to those of the marketing faculties. Is there anyone who will try to prove me wrong? This one investigation helped to prompt me to examine hundreds of the instructor manual questions in many subjects; I'll share more of the specific gems as we move along.

A second study[2] was that of test manuals for six psychology texts. Every fifth question (from a total of almost 2,000) was drawn to be classified independently by two judges. There was almost complete agreement that ninety-five percent of the questions were those requiring recognition of simple information.

Demanding that the questions be on computer tapes may be further indication of an indifferent faculty attitude toward tests. Having questions in a computer means that the entire testing process can become mechanical;

A Test Bank as big as a big city telephone book!

Over 2,000 Questions ■
Weighs 3 lbs. 11 oz. ■
2 inches thick ■
Jumbo 8" x 10" ■

a faculty member only need press a few buttons. As long as tests are primarily for record keeping purposes, I guess this is as good an arrangement as any if the questions are of good quality.

I hope it is becoming clearer and clearer to you that the writing of a multiple-choice question is a very difficult task; I can tell you it is a very time consuming one. Who prepares these tests for instructors' manuals? I have no extensive direct evidence; but in many cases, it is Graduate Teaching Assistants. As I suggested earlier, most of them are not too qualified. I guess many faculty just see testing as a sort of an evil appendage to teaching and are willing to pass it off to others.

I am inclined to think, increasingly, that testing is teaching, in that tests cause substantive learning for the majority of American college students. "Is that going to be on the final?" Faculties, though, of the past quarter century have been numbed by the numbers as they served as personnel selection agents for society. And both students and faculties have been tyrannized by testing.

A young physics professor, when challenged by one of his students about very poor test items--they were unclear, not consistent with the book, and so on--defended himself and the test by saying the items were publisher ones and were, therefore, good.

The Test Bank ad seems to typify attitudes toward tests--large numbers of questions being the sole important criterion. I trust anonymity is preserved because there's no point in singling out one among many.

Cues

Additional prevalent frailties of classroom tests are the cues or tips to correct answers which many multiple-choice and true-false questions contain. Incidentally these cues were not among the inadequacies cited by the Marketing faculties. I'll hazard the guess that most faculties do not know the test cues.

The sophisticated or test-sharp student on the other hand--and there are several--knows what the cues are and consequently makes false positive test scores. That is, such scores reflect the students test-taking ability rather than achievement in that course.

Several of these students in a class result in decreased letter-grade reliabilities, especially if there is grading on the curve. Students who do not know the tricks are penalized. Test-sharp students know more about taking tests than many faculty know about constructing them.

While I did not conduct a statistical investigation, I examined hundreds and hundreds of multiple-choice and true-false items. Some were from fraternity files at several universities, some were supplied by faculty friends, and the remainder were in instructors' manuals accompanying textbooks. Those which follow will acquaint you with construction frailties and the ensuing cues to correct answers. If you are a student, your future course test scores may improve.

The third study[3] of publisher supplied questions was one in which 35 sets of banks as they are called also, for a total of over 26,000 multiple-choice items, were inspected for cues or tips to the correct answers; the questions were those accompanying psychology texts, mainly introductory ones. One-fourth or more of the items in each of 17 sets or banks contained cues of one sort or another and one-third or more of the items in each of ten sets contained cues. Twenty-seven of 35 sets or three-fourths of them contained entirely too many items with cues.

This study is especially suggestive about the extent of poor quality testing—and distressing to me—because psychologists started all this so-called test objectivity and have trumpeted the cult for around 75 years. Yet we violate our own preachments; truly the great washed have little on the great unwashed.

In the main these errors and the resulting cues do not occur in standardized or commercial tests (those produced by the Educational Testing Service, the American College Testing Programs, and others). Professional test builders know better; many faculty and graduate teaching assistants do not. Recall that their test construction skills are acquired via "on my own," "intuition," and "trial and error."

The most frequently occurring cue in classroom multiple-choice tests is the correct alternative or answer being the LONGEST. It tends to be more complete than the others and it may be qualified or explained and is thus longer. I do not mean that the correct answer is always the longest; in a question of good quality, it is not. Because this is the most frequently occurring cue, illustrations of it were given in previous chapters.

1. The agrarian "Granger" Movement of the 1870's, centered largely in the upper Mississippi Valley, led to:*
   a) tough railroad-control legislation
   b) numerous cooperative experiments in the marketing of farm products and in the purchase of machinery and other goods
   c) Civil Service Reform
   d) property-tax relief

---

*Publisher Permissions for questions accompanying textbooks will be found in the Notes and Acknowledgments section. Some of these questions did not accompany textbooks.

2. The value of perfect information is:
   a) the difference between the expected value of the best strategy and the expected value of the poorest.
   b) the expense of a marketing-research project
   c) infinite, because the manager would then make no mistakes
   d) the difference between the expected value of the best strategy and the expected value when the worst decision choices have been avoided by the use of perfect information.

3. Upper Paleolithic art
   a) does not change from one period to the next
   b) is relatively simple, and shows little artistic sophistication
   c) is confined to cave drawings
   d) occurs only during the Magdalenian
   e) shows variation from one period to the next, but it is most sophisticated during the Magdalenian

4. The "ethonographic" present is
   a) the temporal present
   b) the tense anthropologists use in describing a primitive society even if it was written about a hundred years ago and the society no longer exists
   c) from 1492 onward
   d) the time when all the world's cultures were undisturbed by outside influences

5. The CIO sought to recognize
   a) skilled workers
   b) workers without regard for craft lines
   c) agricultural workers
   d) white-collar workers

6. A flexion reflex
   a) causes the sensation of pain to reach the brain when a hot object is touched.
   b) causes a flexing in the triceps when stimulated by impulses.
   c) is simpler than the patellar reflex.
   d) causes an inhibitory neuron to release transmitter which hyperpolarizes the meter neurons of the triceps.
   e) none of these

7. How does a crustacean skeletal muscle differ from the vertebrate skeletal muscle?
   a) one lacks mitochondria; the other does not
   b) vertebrate muscle is striated; crustacean muscle is smooth
   c) crustacean muscle is controlled by stimulatory and inhibitory nerves directly; vertebrate muscle is directly controlled only by excitatory nerves.
   d) actin is absent in crustacean muscles
   e) none of the above

8. A productive corn field
   a) is an example of a climax ecosystem.
   b) is a human-manipulated system to partition more solar energy into edible materials.
   c) illustrates the role of plants as consumers.
   d) all of the above are correct
   e) none of the above is correct

9. Photosynthesis
   a) is normally 40 percent efficient.
   b) is a sequence of reactions that produces high energy sugars from low-energy substances.
   c) involves the direct alternatives of herbivores.
   d) all of the above are correct.
   e) none of the above is correct.

Other major cues, and ones that also occur quite frequently, are those in which there are certain RESEMBLANCES--sometimes glaringly obvious--between the alternatives or answers and an aspect of the stem or question.

10. The average number of years lived by each member of a population is:
    a) a crude death rate.
    b) average life expectancy.
    c) crude birth rate.
    d) none of the above.

11. The passage of individuals from one social position to another is:
    a) social mobility
    b) occupational mobility
    c) economic mobility
    d) political mobility

12. It appears that the next step in the marketing revolution will be:
    a) financially oriented companies
    b) better promotional efforts
    c) marketing companies
    d) more aggressive sales

13. The use of specialized "boxes" for protection and easy handling of goods in storage and transit refers to:
    a) the distribution center concept
    b) the bill of lading
    c) making bulk
    d) containerization

14. The ability of a microorganism to enter the body and to spread throughout the tissues can be defined as:
    a) infectivity
    b) invasiveness
    c) toxicity
    d) virulence

15. A study in which neither the investigator nor the subjects knows which group the subject has been assigned to is known as a:
    a) Latin square design
    b) randomized blocks design
    c) double blind design
    d) Lindquist Type I design

The next three questions illustrate RESEMBLANCE cues deriving from foreign language vocabularies; in this first one, a student need know only that lipoma means fat (Greek):

16. A tumor of the buccal mucosa histologically showing predominantly adult fat would best be described as a(an):
    a) epulis
    b) lipoma
    c) choristoma
    d) nodular fasciitis
    e) Von Recklinghausin's disease

In this next one, students do not even need to know the Greek origin of water--hydro; thoughtful ones will think of hydrant and hydro-electric:

17. Hydrophylic molecules tend to associate with:
    a) water
    b) proteins
    c) phospholipids
    d) all of these
    e) none of these

Surely most college students associate oxygen with air and breathing and maybe with the Latin "pulmo."

18. This is the only <u>vein</u> in the human body that transports <u>oxygenated blood</u>:
   a) aorta vein
   <u>b)</u> pulmonary vein
   c) superior vena cava
   d) coronary vein
   e) cardiac vein

   This next question contains, not one, but two cues: RESEMBLANCE and LONGEST (an explanation is given in the correct alternative and not in the others). It is from a very advanced test. Most students got it right--25 of 27. But why? Did they <u>know</u> the answer or go by the cues?

19. The major goal of surgical therapy in a patient with a ruptured intracranial aneurysm is:
   <u>a)</u> repair of the aneurysm to prevent further bleeding
   b) drainage of the bloody spinal fluid
   c) resection of the mass
   d) control of the hydrocephalus
   e) none of the above

   Much less common, but worth watching for, is the cue of the correct alternative being very DIFFERENT from the others. Note:

20. The idea that man in his natural state is a "noble savage" is attributed to:
   a) Thomas Hobbes
   b) Charles Darwin
   <u>c)</u> Jean Jacques Rousseau
   d) Franz Boas

21. The leading coal producing area of the U.S.S.R. is:
   a) Ural area
   b) Tula area
   c) Kuznetsk area
   <u>d)</u> Donets basin

22. Union membership between 1896 and 1910
   a) declined by fifty percent
   b) declined slightly
   c) increased slightly
   <u>d)</u> increased three-fold

   Sometimes a cue to the answer to a later question is given in a PREVIOUS question:

23. A group that comes together for a common purpose is:
    a) a public
    b) a mob
    c) a mass
    d) none of the above

24. The Ku Klux Klan can be considered a _____ during their cross burning ceremonies
    a) casual crowd
    b) an expressive crowd
    c) mob
    d) conventional crowd

An additional cue in this one is GRAMMATICAL errors. The test-sharp student eliminates alternative "b" because it is grammatically incorrect in relation to the stem. Not only are "a" and "an" often giveaways, but sometimes verb tense discrepancies between the stem and an alternative are tip-offs.

25. Which of the following apraxias lateralize most consistently to the dominant hemisphere?
    a) constructional apraxia
    b) buccal-lingual apraxia
    c) gait apraxia
    d) ideomotor apraxia
    e) both b and d

With the plural "apraxias" in the stem, quite obviously only one of the alternatives "e" is plural and therefore the correct answer or choice.

While not so common in multiple-choice items, although they do occur therein, ABSOLUTES--all, never, always, and others--almost always render an alternative incorrect. In a true-false item, they tend to render the item false.

26. All things in the universe can be studied by the scientific method.
27. It is impossible for two different groups to coexist peacefully in the same area.
28. Prejudice always leads to discrimination.
29. Levels of fertility are the same for all segments of the U.S. population.
30. All disasters can be and are expected events.
31. Opportunities to socialize on the job are important to everyone.

I trust you studied these cues and the examples carefully--a multiple-choice test about the cues awaits you. This type test will be used because it requires the mental activity of recognition; I hope you learn to recognize the cues in other multiple-choice questions. The test you will take is an illustration of one that is sync with learning objectives or aims.

There are six major cues:
1) The LONGEST alternative
2) RESEMBLANCES between a portion of the stem and the correct alternative
3) an alternative strikingly DIFFERENT from the others
4) an answer being contained in a PREVIOUS item
5) GRAMMATICAL errors
6) ABSOLUTES

There are also the indirect cues of "all of the above" and "none of the above" as alternatives. "All of the above" increases the chances of students guessing the correct answer. When only one choice is to be made, if they note that two of the alternatives are correct, then "all of the above" is probably correct. The alternative "all of the above" is incorrect, of course, if one of the remaining alternatives is incorrect.

"None of the above" as an alternative is often a filler--the writer of the item can't think of anything else. When it is, the test-sharp student is likely to detect it. For a four-alternative question, the odds of guessing correctly then increase from 4/1 to 3/1.

In one instructor's manual with 366 five-alternative multiple-choice questions, one-third of them contained both "all of the above" and "none of the above." In almost half of these pairs, "all of the above" was the correct choice. An additional one-fifth of all the items contained either one or the other as alternatives. Thus around half the multiple-choice questions in this one manual contained these indirect cues.

Finally, I have not meant to imply that multiple-choice questions should not be used. Good quality ones--valid and reliable--are most appropriate. But a great deal of time is required for their creation.

Odd behavior was observed of a new college graduate at a special celebration cocktail party. When asked a question by the host, he would answer only "True" or "False." When pressed for details, he would reply either "A" or "B" or "C" or merely "none of the above." Otherwise he remained mute.

Most of the emphasis thus far has been on multiple-choice questions because they are the ones which are seductively misleading for both faculty and students. It is my hope that essay questions will enjoy a revival; it is time to lift the misguided ban.

The intellectual demands of essay questions upon students far exceed those of multiple-choice ones with their limited focus on the recognition of predetermined and narrowly correct answers. Essay questions require students to decide, first, what to say (in important issues, no small task) and second, how to say it.

"How to say it" entails, at a minimum, correct usage of the English language, choosing words carefully and precisely, and some coherent ordering of thoughts. These attributes should be utilized by a student in demonstrating the attainment of these and other course objectives--comprehension or understanding of course material, applying that material in other contexts, and perhaps most importantly, evaluating or judging its worth. This would include the citing of evidence to support a conclusion.

Deciding what to say and how to say it helps to develop clarity of thought. Comprehending and applying and evaluating cannot be useful to students unless expressed clearly and effectively either orally or in writing. Faculties cannot assist in the development of clarity of thought unless there is some overt manifestation of it.

I would insist that quality of thought is demonstrated by quality of expression. And one thing is certain: Both require practice and practice accompanied by constructive criticisms. A freshman course in composition, no matter how good, is not enough.

A few years ago, seniors at Dartmouth College were required to write themes about some pressing issue. Their papers were then compared with those of freshmen at the end of their composition course. A meticulously objective scoring system was followed and each paper was marked for eight types of errors: focus and structure, material, paragraphs, sentences, words, grammar, punctuation and mechanics, and spelling. The seniors made from twice to ten times as many errors per catagory as did the freshmen.

There is no doubt in my mind that students do not write as well now as they did, say 20 years ago--this indictment includes graduate students. One major explanation here is that students have not been answering essay questions. Let me repeat---tests are powerful determinants of learning. If writing isn't required, students won't consider learning to do so important.

I remind you, too, that high school students receive little significant practice in writing. There is no way that English teachers, no matter how capable and dedicated, can provide detailed constructive criticism (feedback) when they have between 25 and 35 students in each of four or five classes per day five days per week. As a nation, do we really believe our propaganda about the necessity for improving communication?

Now there is much more to preparing essay questions--especially those seeking quality of thought as well as quality of expression--than dashing them off in a hurry. These (which appeared in previous chapters) illustrate how they should not be written; all are of poor quality:

<u>Chapter 1.</u> -- Since we know how bad inflation is, why is it that we are not now, and have not since 1972, brought inflation rates down to acceptable levels?
<u>Chapter 2.</u> -- Write a few lines on: 1) I.Q., 2) Evolution, 3) The Scientific Method, 4) Role and Status, 5) Instinct and Learned Behavior.
<u>Chapter 3.</u> -- What is the urban transportation problem and what are its causes?
<u>Chapter 4.</u> -- Discuss the need for 'governments' with respect to the 'public good'.
<u>Chapter 5.</u> -- (newly appearing) Discuss the concept of 'The New South'.

All of these are very poor quality questions, primarily because they are entirely too broad in scope. Moreover, each one of them appeared with several other questions on a regular 50-minute exam. The one, "Write a few lines on . . .", is particularly onerous; I believe it is the worst I have encountered.

These questions encourage, yea demand, psyching the prof; that is, students are forced to try to guess what is wanted in an answer. You, of course, recognize that a book or books can be written about any of these questions. This breadth is one of the reasons students "shoot the breeze"-- they try to increase their odds of saying at least some of the things which are wanted. Just where does one start in answering any of those questions?

But "shooting the breeze" is poor quality of expression which, in turn, reflects poor quality of thought. At the same time, it is all but impossible to grade such answers fairly or reliably. It is very poor questions such as these which have given essay items such a bad name. With better quality questions, we can demand clarity of expression and the papers can be graded with much better consistency.

Here now are a few very high quality questions. Each one of them is from an exam on which there were three questions; students were given 90 minutes to complete all three. The questions are explicit enough so that a student does not have to guess about how to cover the universe.

Individual organisms make short-term adjustments to temporary environmental changes in temperature, moisture, light, or the chemical environment. Choose ANY ONE of these enironmental factors and describe mechanisms by which a) animals and b) plants may adjust to changes in that factor.

The overall equation for aerobic respiration is usually written as the reverse of the overall equation for photosyntheses. What features of the biochemical pathways involved in the two processes are the reverse of one another and what features are not?

The immune responses of organisms involve antigens, antibodies, and other factors. Describe the <u>immune response</u> and discuss its role in THREE of the following phenomena.

a) Blood transfusions   c) Disease resistance
b) Rh incompatability   d) Tissue transplants

During development in multicellular organisms, the cells become different from one another, even though they possess a common genetic heritage. Describe experiments in several organisms which explore the problem of differentiation at the gene level, the cell level, or the tissue level, and discuss how these experiments have aided our understanding of development.

Each year a number of children are born with biological defects that impair normal function. For THREE of the following conditions, discuss such aspects as the biological cause, the methods of treatment, and possible means of detection and/or prevention.

a) Phenylketonia (PKU)   e) Erythoblastosis fetalis
b) Sickle cell anemia   f) Blue-baby condition
c) Down's syndrome (Mongolism)   g) "Tay-Sachs"
d) Cretinism

Controversy has surrounded the development of many biological concepts. State the contrasting viewpoints for three of the following. Then discuss the evidence from reasoning, observations, or an experiment that led to the currently accepted resolution of the issue.

   a) Are genes made up chemically of proteins or DNA?
   b) Are evolutionary changes best explained by the Lamarckian or the Darwinian theory?
   c) Is the oxygen by-product of photosynthesis derived form carbon dioxide or from water?
   d) If a reducing atmosphere is assumed to have existed on the primitive Earth, were the first forms of life autotrophic or heterotrophic?

Human beings have altered the environment in a number of ways. Discuss the beneficial and harmful modifications of the environment brought about by the use of the following:

   a) Nuclear energy
   b) Fertilizers and pesticides
   c) Fossil fuels and metals.

Charles Darwin's theory of natural selection had a significant influence on the understanding of the evolution of organisms. Discuss each of the following:

   a) the importance of Darwin's voyage on the H.M.S. Beagle to the development of his theory;
   b) the major points proposed by Darwin in this theory;
   c) two major determinants in Darwin's theory that stem from modern findings.*

These next questions are history ones. Note the very exact directions to the students and note, too, the limits imposed by the time period.

Time -- 45 minutes

Directions: You are to answer ONE of the following five questions. Carefully choose the question which you are best prepared to answer in 45 minutes. Be sure to cite relevant historical evidence to substantiate your generalizations and to illustrate your answer. Make certain to number your answer as the question is numbered below.

---

*The above essay questions and the history ones which follow were reprinted by permission of Educational Testing Service, the copyright owner.

1. "Most reform legislation since 1900 has been the work of special interests seeking to advance their own well-being, but the adoption of such legislation has required the general support of others who were not directly affected but who perceived it to be in the public interest."

   Assess the validity of this statement with reference to THREE examples of reform legislation since 1900. You may draw your examples from reform at any level of government: national, state, or municipal.

2. "American social reform movements from 1820 to 1860 were characterized by unyielding perfectionism, impatience with compromise, and distrust of established social institutions. These qualities explain the degree of success or failure of these movements in achieving their objectives."

   Discuss with reference to both antislavery and ONE other reform movement of the period 1820-1860 (for example, temperance, women's rights, communitarianism, prison reform, or educational reform).

3. "During the seventeenth century and increasingly in the eighteenth century, British colonists in America charged Great Britain with violating the ideals of rule of law, self-government, and, ultimately, equality of rights. Yet the colonists themselves violated these ideals in their treatment of blacks, American Indians (Native Americans), and even poorer classes of white settlers."

   Assess the validity of this view.

4. "Between 1776 and 1823 a young and weak United States achieved considerable success in foreign policy when confronted with the two principal European powers, Great Britain and France. Between 1914 and 1950, however, a far more powerful United States was far less successful in achieving its foreign policy objectives in Europe."

   Discuss by comparing United States foreign policy during the period 1776-1823, with United States policy in Europe during ONE of the following periods: 1914-1932 or 1933-1950.

5. "During the twentieth century, American 'progressives' or 'liberals' at some times advocated a strong presidency and

expanded executive power, while 'conservatives' opposed the expansion of these powers. At other times the 'liberal' and 'conservative' positions were reversed."

Assess the validity of this statement with reference to the periods 1900-1940 <u>and</u> 1965-1974.

These questions were taken from the well-established and successful Advanced Placement Examinations. In 1980, for example, around 120,000 high school seniors seeking college credits took one or more of them. The Advanced Placement Exams are designed to enable students to demonstrate their command of a full year's work in a given subject.

Prior to administration, precise scoring standards are devised and graders are trained so as to promote uniformity and impartiality. These are the procedures for seeking scoring reliability. As you may recall, from earlier chapters, lack of reliability was a major reason for the decline in the use of essay tests.

The very act of thinking through a question during its preparation and what sorts of answers are wanted from students are important first steps a faculty member can take toward reliability of scoring. Having the question judged by a colleague prior to its use is still another action in that direction; such a review will help to eliminate ambiguities and awkward phrases.

After the test, several procedures will help to minimize errors in marking. All cues to identification of the owner of a paper should be removed; at the least names should be deleted. All Number 1 questions should be marked before proceeding to the Number 2's, and so on.

These two procedures are ways of dealing with the very bothersome "halo effect." This is no time for the overall impression of a student--be it positive or negative--to influence marking judgment. Nor should the answer to a given question influence the graders reactions to other answers of the same student.

Note the absence from the Advanced Placement questions of "Do you believe. . .?", "Do you think. . .?", "In your opinion. . . ." There are only personal standards by which to judge the answers to these sorts of questions and those are not pertinent to course material.

Time consuming? Yes! Is the preparation of multiple-choice questions time consuming? Yes!

In the final analysis, all good quality testing is time consuming!

6

Where To?

College classroom testing is an ubiquitous enterprise. Millions have participated in and been touched by classroom tests and millions more will be affected in the future. Almost all participants have been content, judging by their silence, with the testing process; some, on the other hand, have been discontented with the test products--the ABCDF symbols! The discontent is manifested by a few students who complain that their grades are too low and by periodic public manifestos bemoaning grade inflation. We are numbed by the numbers.

Occasionally a student will vow that upon graduation, steps will be taken to correct certain evil inequities. And occasionally parents will declare that once a grade problem of their son or daughter is resolved, they will see to it that preventive corrective action will be taken. Little or nothing comes of these declarations.

There are no simple routes to improving college classroom tests. Challenging the process rather than the products is a novel idea and considerable time will be required to become accustomed to it. With so many people involved and with some of them believing that the products are inviolable, no matter how they have been derived, it is easy for none to take responsibility for alterations. Furthermore, grades are such comfortable currency for many, that tampering with the base of the edifice will be viewed as threatening and thus resisted.

Certain guiding principles have evolved for college classroom testing-- the primary one being that giving tests in courses is part of teaching and as such is protected by the shield of academic freedom. Translated, this has meant that individual faculty members pursue all aspects of teaching as they see fit. The protection means, too, that college and university administrators--presidents, chancellors, deans, and assorted assistants--as well as colleagues, keep hands off.

It would be easy for me to recommend that institutions of higher learning adopt special policies designed to correct some of the evils I have exposed. If I did so, with rare exception, nothing would happen within most of the several thousand colleges and universities, because of faculty indifference and adherence to certain misunderstood tenets of academic freedom.

"Academic freedom" is often an automatic thoughtless protective cry (as are "free enterprise" and "interference with the doctor-patient relationship"), but heeded nonetheless. Inaction would be true especially in the behemoth universities--those with enrollments of 20,000 plus. Academic freedom also means license to many; in this instance license to be allowed to give poor quality tests to their students.

Yet the major problems are within those factories, if for no other reason than the fact that therein are the largest numbers of students who are being affected adversely. And therein is where the publishers push the books (for obvious reasons) with the twisted test questions.

The two principle sets of participants in the testing enterprise are professors and students; the primary burden of promoting test improvements falls upon them. Since students outnumber their mentors and since students are the victims, students should be the leaders in pushing for reforms.

It is fortunate for the cause that the ages of college students today extend beyond the usual 18-21 group; around one-third are 25 and over. Older students are less likely to be aiming for professional schools and as a consequence can be less concerned about faculty retaliation via losses of hundredths of GPA points.

I do believe that the tactic most likely to succeed is persuasion! Most faculty are reasonable people and if approached properly will respond favorably to reason. Many of them are just plain unaware of certain problems with classroom tests. But their attention must be caught--and this will require some dramatics.

In the first place it is hard to catch the attention of busy people and in the second place there is not only faculty complacency but self-satisfaction. A recent study,[1] by the Center for the Study of Higher Education at the University of Michigan, revealed that 90 percent of faculties in 24 institutions rated themselves above average as teachers and that almost 30 percent of these judged themselves to be superior.

These smug self-assessments were true to equal degrees in community colleges, and both public and private universities. In contrast, these people rated less than 10 percent of their departmental colleagues as superior. It's always the other person who needs to improve. My suggestions for dramatics may be rather feeble, that is, they may not be sufficiently potent, but they may stimulate others to greater heights.

Well! Three groups of people on a given campus, working separately and jointly, can bring about improvements in classroom tests. These people are I) members of the several student organizations, II) individual students in courses, and III) already interested and concerned faculty.

I. Student organizations, for example, student government, can mount campaigns through their own members to collect actual poor quality tests and poor quality questions. These can then be published in the student newspaper as a way of informing an entire campus about poor quality testing. Such groups must not copy examples from this book; if they do their cause will be harmed. Items will be most effective in arousing awareness if they are local and personal.

Organizations should have no trouble in finding gems such as these:

T-F: Fiscal policy influences economic activity in the economy.

An individual should secure the assistance of a _____ when preparing a will.

Since we know how bad inflation is, why is it that we are not now and have not since 1972, brought inflation rates down to acceptable levels?

Tradition has it that the Compromise of 1877 was worked out:
a) by President Ulysses S. Grant
b) between Hayes and Tilden
c) at the Wormley Hotel
d) both a and c

A major defense of colleges and universities when being challenged (other organizations are no exception) is something to the effect: "Now that may be true at the University of _____ but not here." Similarly within an institution, the defense goes something like: "Oh, I've seen some of the tests in the _____ Department and they are terrible, but in my department. . . ." Finally, individuals react in like manner: "I've heard all sorts of complaints about Professor _____'s tests; now mine are. . . ."

So make your reports about tests local. If you use illustrations from this book or from other campuses, the defensive retort will be: "There, not here. . ." Use the poor quality questions in this book only as guides--you can find plenty of similar poor quality on your own campus. Incidentally, an excellent source of material is fraternity files--and many of them are up-to-date; old questions will provoke defensiveness, also. The student newspaper might plan a series of articles over the period of an academic year with the theme THE TERRIBLE TESTS HERE.

In the meantime seek out your local examination office. These are to be found on many large campuses and a few small ones and go by such names as Measurement Service Center, Division of Examination Service, Measurement and Research Center, Measurement and Evaluation Center, and others. The people who staff these shops are real test experts and will be ready and able to provide all sorts of help for your campaign and to faculties. By and large, faculties do not seek assistance for test construction from these offices.

The fact that the services of these offices are not sought is further evidence for my claim of indifferent attitudes of faculties. Some of these offices have been operating for many years; the majority of faculty on a big campus do not even know of the existence of such a shop. If your school does not have one of these shops, visit the Psychology Department or the Educational Psychology Department. More than likely you will find a test specialist in one of those places who will be glad to assist you.

II. The second group, individual students in courses, can make contributions by collecting real live test questions and by asking questions of individual faculty about the tests they take. Now here's where we must proceed with caution, care, and cunning. There are ways of asking questions of faculty about their tests which will arouse nothing but ire and resentment--ignominious defeat of interrogators will result. On the other hand, there are ways of approaching faculty that will increase the odds of favorable action. Be assertive, but not aggressive.

So, here are the main do's and don'ts for those of you who will participate in this campaign--THE TERRIBLE TESTS HERE!

1) Never be one of those who asks in class "Is this going to be on the final?" or "Is the test going to be objective or essay?" If you ask either of those questions, you will be marked and your intentions no matter how noble, will be highly suspect.

2) Do not ask questions about test quality in class; make an office appointment with the professor.

3) Do not go to the office alone--have one or two other students in the same course go with you. If you go alone, you are an easy target for being seen as just another disgruntled student with an isolated gripe. It is easy for a faculty member to intimidate a lone student. Two or three students sort of outnumber a single professor and provide moral support for each other.

4) Before the meeting review the material about reliability and validity in this book, and be sure you understand it. Test your understanding by explaining the two concepts to other students. Now here's the reason I introduced those two technical terms--technical terms are used by experts

to confuse the opposition, to obfuscate the issues, and to make themselves appear learned. So when facing an expert in some field, use other technical terms that the person does not know.

As a matter of fact, consult your examination office or a test specialist on the faculty before the visit. All of those people will be enormously helpful in sharpening your understanding, giving you confidence, and so on. They can probably give you some local ammunition.

5) After the usual social amenities and a statement about how wonderful the course is and how much you are learning, ask something to the effect "Please explain to us about how this test fits the objectives of the course" or "Please tell us about how valid this test is and how you determined the validity of it." Listen politely and ask for clarification if needed; it will be and not because of your inadequacies.

6) Now please tell us about the reliabilities of your tests. "What method do you use--test-retest, split-half, or what?" "Just what is the coefficient of reliability of this last test?" Around three-fourths or more of your subjects won't have the faintest idea of what you're asking. Another exceptionally good off-balance question is "What was the standard error of measurement for your final?"

Most of your faculty subjects are going to be thoroughly stunned; first because you did not come seeking points to be added to your test score, and second because they will not be able to explain the concepts of validity, reliability, and associated issues. Your mission will have been accomplished anyway; you will have gotten attention within the context of THE TERRIBLE TESTS HERE.

You might want to leave a few book references with them; your examination center or faculty test specialist can provide several excellent ones. If your interviewee has been somewhat recalcitrant ask, "Are you familiar with the decision of the United States Supreme Court in Griggs vs. Duke Power Company?"[2] This was a 1971 case in which the Court declared that tests and degrees are not fixed measures of ability. The Court ruled that tests must not be controlling forces in personnel decisions, unless they have been demonstrated to be reasonable measures.

III. The third group, interested faculty, can not only provide moral support for all students who seek it, they can begin to seek the creation of certain testing policies in academic departments. (Here's another example of local and personal activity). I believe that profound improvements would occur in classroom tests by the simple expedient of all questions being edited by a colleague before their administration. This--in my view--should become institutional policy. At the very least, ambiguous wording and awkward phrasing would be reduced.

The already interested faculty are the ones to begin a crusade for better quality questions to accompany textbooks. These faculty can analyze carefully any of the questions they may be using and can encourage their colleagues in other academic fields to do likewise. Detailed statistical reports including such matters as the number of questions in a specific manual containing answer cues could be rendered to textbook authors and to their publishers.

All the while, off-campus groups need not be idle; publishers above all. They can conduct analyses of their own products, begin to purify what has already been produced, and take steps to sin no more. The examination centers just mentioned have many knowledgeable people who can provide aid to them. Just as publishers are proud of the books they produce, they should be proud of the test items. The weight and thickness of a test manual are laughable criteria.

One publisher, Harper and Row, Inc., has taken important steps to improve questions. It has created an advisory committee, composed of members of the company and faculty consultants, to provide guidance in the creation of textbook questions. A special manual has been prepared for item authors, and all questions will be reviewed by at least one test authority before they are released.

Recruiters for business and industry can make contributions by asking to see copies of tests which have been used in particular courses. Those seeking accountants, for example, might ask to see copies of exams from the Accounting Department. A glance would tell the experienced recruiter whether the tests had gotten at mental trivia or something of a higher order.

I don't have much hope for this suggestion, but grade-point-averages should be removed from all transcripts before they are released to the public. As I indicated earlier, there are numerous ways of calculating GPA's and the way of a given institution is not always made clear. If a company or a graduate school wants a number let that outfit derive it; the composition of it will then be known.

I'm confident that most viewers of transcripts look at the grade-point-average _first_--that uni-dimensional symbol of multi-dimensional phenomena- and are biased by it immediately. If that number isn't there, viewers would be forced to examine the entire record. Here's a project for the American Association of Collegiate Registrars and Admissions Officers. We are numbed by the numbers.

For those immediate endeavors, I hope several philanthropic foundations are ready to provide appropriate sums of money to support the time-consuming campaigns on several major campuses. Since the federal

Fund for the Improvement of Postsecondary Education, better known as FIPSE, is action oriented, I can't think of a better national project for it than that of promoting the improvement of classroom tests.

My final suggestion must be a very long-range one; because it defies several hundred years of tradition, it will be resisted most vigorously--"In the year of our Lord, 1432. . . ." I refer to instructor autonomy, that is, the almost universal practice of tests and grades in a given course being entirely under the control of one lone instructor. I believe this practice has many subtly pervasive deleterious influences.

The individual instructor serves in two opposing capacities: on the one hand helping students learn, and on the other serving as judge and jury. The combining of these two functions tends to inhibit the development of certain desirable qualities in students. As one illustration, most students do not learn to ask informed questions. Yet one very crucial skill for an educated citizen and worker is that of using informed questions to challenge the assertions of experts and authorities.

All experts wear blinders, suffer knowledge deficiencies, and have vested interests. Questioning them is extraordinarily difficult because one must know the questions to ask and also because they are very skillful in avoiding that which they wish to avoid. I overheard a citizen, who wanted to know if he would be paying higher taxes, ask a small town manager: "Is the tax rate going up next year?" The manager answered emphatically (and truthfully) "No," but he did not answer completely. He failed to tell that tax assessments were being increased; this would mean higher taxes. The citizen asked the wrong question.

A senator was asked on television about certain Federal crop subsidies in his home state; he denied their existence. Later in the program, by accident, it was revealed that there were crop supports. The correspondent had asked the wrong question initially; the senator was thereby able to evade the intent of the query.

Because of the highly developed personnel-selection function of colleges and universities (detailed in Chapter 1) an instructor possesses awesome power. In most institutions the instructor has sole responsibility for testing and grading and is the sole arbiter if there are challenges. Even in some schools where there are academic grievance committes, such bodies can only recommend that corrective actions be taken for faculty testing errors. Students are keenly aware of this power and tread lightly; they do not dare to jeopardize a grade by offending or threatening a faculty member.

In 1977, 13 students at Southern Oregon State College[3] were forced to seek redress in the courts because the President, two faculty members, and the Registrar refused to obey the edict of a duly authorized college committee for hearing academic grievances. The students had received Incompletes as their grades; they felt the I's were unjustified. The Grievance Committee ruled that the Incompletes had been assigned arbitrarily and capriciously and ordered that the grades be changed. The four college officials refused to honor the edict of it's own Committee.

Is it any wonder that students do not question the academic assertions of, or disagree with, the experts with whom they have frequent contacts? Yet question asking skills need to be practiced if they are to be developed.

Almost all course tests demand answers to questions posed by the instructor. Students might be helped in developing their reasoning abilities if some tests asked them to frame important questions rather than to supply inherited answers. Students must conclude that all the questions and all the answers are known.

Another reason for the growing importance of question asking is the accelerating number of stuffy, pretentious assertions. By design, messages are not always clear. The National Bureau of Standards declared it would study the "thermal, visual, and acoustical benefits of fenestration." The title for a new standardized test is "Measurement of Aptitude for Divergent Verbal Productions." A psychologist defined "practice or drill" (as in "to practice the piano"): "repetitive experience designed to solidify a learned response."

A query to the Department of Interior was answered thusly:

> The loss of wildlife-wetland habitat in the Nebraska sandhills has been defined as an IRP and has been ranked #52 in our list of national concerns. It ranks #5 in our list of concerns for region 6. Once suggested alternatives have been developed, we then review the IRP and strategy plan. An EIS will not be prepared on Sandlands wetland production after such reviews.

It is my impression that most people do not question authorities. And while I do not mean to imply that poor quality tests are the sole causes of such passivity and undue reliance on the pronouncement of others, I do believe that tests contribute.

At the same time many of the few who do question the experts do so in a belligerent fashion. Experts are often such masters at fending off attack that little satisfaction results. Again, more attention to wise question-asking in college might hlep.

But to continue with my academic heresy, one way of dampening instructor autonomy is via separating the teaching and testing functions. This, too, would be a major route to improving classroom tests. This idea is not original. The two functions were separated in one division of the University of Chicago[4] in 1931--fifty years ago; the program was a success for almost 25 years.

In creating the Board of Examinations the university wished, first, to separate the teaching and testing functions of individual faculty members. It was believed that the two functions interfered with each other. A second reason was the desire to have students assume increasing responsibility for decisions made about their undergraduate education. It was hoped that having requirements for graduation expressed in terms of examinations to be completed would help students assume responsibility about such matters as attending class and amount of studying. The third goal was that of improving the quality of classroom tests. College classroom testing was in the same state of disarray then as now. Of course, there were many fewer students--around one million.

Staff members of the Board and the faculty worked together very closely in developing the course tests. This included visits to classes by the examiners and all questions being edited by the faculty before their use. The reliabilities for the tests were very high, even better than those for many standardized tests of today (for benefit of the statistically minded, the coefficients varied between .90 and .95).

There was major concern about test validities. In seeming contrast to today, the faculty wished to test for much more than recognition of isolated information. The faculty wished to have tests which tapped objectives of the courses, and the Board of Examinations was pushed to secure evidence about these matters.

Thus numerous studies about validities were conducted and the tests were improved constantly. There were circular positive effects--faculty members were forced to be clear about their objectives and this clarity, in turn, resulted in more valid tests.

Reasons for the demise of this examination program are not clear, but one reason seems to have been the departure of Robert Maynard Hutchins, the boy wonder president from 1929 through 1945.

To my knowledge, the only other instance of separating the teaching and testing functions is the Honors Program of Swarthmore College.[5] During the junior and senior years, students pursue their studies either independently or in small seminars. At the end of the senior year, each student is subjected to a three-hour written examination and to an oral examination in each subject. The written exams are prepared and evaluated by faculty members from other institutions and the oral ones are conducted by visitors also.

Both alumni and faculty maintain that the system helps to create an atmosphere of faculty-student collaboration; it is as though faculty members and students work together to meet and impress a sort of common foe, the visiting examiner. You can be sure home faculty are challenged by students about many of their academic assertions.

It is my fervent hope that no one will even think of any sort of legislation designed to bring about alterations (as is happening for commercial tests), either state or national. Legalizing will only make matters worse; efforts in that direction will arouse massive faculty resistance--and properly so.

At the same time, classroom testing laws would interfere with the complexities of college and university environments wherein we are attempting to promote diverse and varied learning. For the welfare of the nation these complexities must remain unfettered. I have focused upon written tests because they are the most common by far, but other test types are used--and must continue to be.

Test Prayer

Now I lay me down to study,
I pray the Lord I won't go nutty,
If I should fail to learn this junk,
I pray the Lord I will not flunk.
But if I do, don't pity me at all,
Just lay my bones down in the study hall;
Tell my teacher I did my best,
Then pile my books upon my chest.
Now I lay me down to rest
And pray I'll pass tomorrow's test.
If I should die before I wake,
That's one less test I'll have to take.
                    Sufferin' Student (author unknown)

THE PROMISED TEST[6]

The multiple-choice questions on the next page (do not look) can be answered solely with your newly acquired knowledge about test cues or tips. Each of six questions has one and only one correct answer.

Before turning the page list the numbers 1, 2, 3, 4, 5, 6 down the page on a separate sheet of paper. Put your answers on that separate sheet by writing the letter of the correct alternative (a or b or c or d) by the number for that question. I suggested you mark your answers on a separate sheet of paper so that you can then have other people take the test.

TURN THE PAGE and demonstrate your knowledge.

THE TEST

1. Trassig normally occurs when the
   a. dissels frull.
   b. lusp chasses the vom.
   c. belgo lisks easily.
   d. viskal flans, if the viskal is zortil.

2. The fribbled breg will snicker best with an
   a. Mors.
   b. Ignu.
   c. Cerst.
   d. Sortar.

3. What probable causes are indicated when tristal doss occurs in a compots?
   a. The sabs foped and the doths tinzed.
   b. The kredges roted with the rots.
   c. Rakogs were not accepted in the sluth.
   d. Polats were thonced in the sluth.

4. The primary purpose of the cluss in frumpaling is to
   a. remove cluss-prangs.
   b. patch tremalls.
   c. loosen cloughs.
   d. repair plumots.

5. Why does the sigla frequently overfesk the trelsum?
   a. All siglas are mellious.
   b. Siglas are always votial.
   c. The trelsum is usually tarious.
   d. No trelsa are directly feskable.

6. The snickering function of the Ignu is most effectively performed in connection with which one of the following snicker snacks?
   a. Arazma tol.
   b. Fribbled breg.
   c. Groshed stantol.
   d. Frallied stantol.

Answers will be found at the end of Appendix A.

Notes and Acknowledgments

1

The Footlish Fetish

1. Hofstadter, R: Anti-Intellectualism in American Life. NY, Vintage Books, 1966, p. 339.

2. Hoffman, Banesh: The Tyranny of Testing. NY, Crowell-Collier, 1962. This book reappeared in paperback in 1978.

3. Black, Hillel: They Shall Not Pass. NY, Wm. Morrow, 1963.

4. Strenio, Andrew: The Testing Trap. NY, Rawson, Wade, 1979.

5. Cited in Skager, Rodney: On the use and importance of tests of ability in admission to postsecondary education. Los Angeles, Univ. Calif., 1980. (Multilithed.)

6. Page, Ellis Batten: Teacher comments and student performance: A seventy-four classroom experiment in school motivation. J Educ Psych, 49(4): 173-181, 1958.

7. Sassenrath, Julius M., and Gaverick, Charles M.: Effects of differential feedback from examinations on retention and transfer. J Educ Psych, 56(5): 259-263, 1965.

8. Karraker, R. J.: Knowledge of results and incorrect recall of plausible multiple-choice alternatives. J Educ Psych, 58(1): 11-14, 1967.

9. Hodgkinson, Harold, Walter, William, and Coover, Robert: Bard corrects freshmen themes on tape. AAHE Coll Univ Bull, 20(10): 2-3, 1968.

10. Fisher, K., Williams, S., and Roth, J.: Qualitative and quantitative differences in learning associated with frequent multiple-choice testing. Davis, Univ. Calif., 1980. (Multilithed.)

11. The author is unknown; the piece appeared in Forbes Magazine, September 15, 1969.

12. Cited in Munn, N. L.: Introduction to Psychology. Boston, Houghton-Mifflin, 1962. Reprinted by permission of Houghton-Mifflin Co.

13. Hoyt, D. P.: The Relationship Between College Grades and Adult Achievement. Iowa City, American College Testing Program, 1965.

14. McClelland, David C.: Testing for competence rather than for "intelligence". Am Psych, 28(1): 1-14, 1973.

15. Berg, Ivar: Education and Jobs: The Great Training Robbery. NY, Praeger, 1970.

16. Nelson, A. M.: Undergraduate academic achievement in college as an indicator of occupational success, Professional Series PS-75-5. Washington, D. C., U. S. Civil Service Commission, Bureau of Policies and Standards, Department of Commerce, 1975.

17. Collins, Janet R., and Nickel, Kenneth N.: Grading policies in higher education: The Kansas study/The national survey. Wichita State Univ Bull, University Studies 103, 51: 5-57, 1975.

18. See Rowntree, Derek: Assessing Students: How Shall We Know Them? NY, Harper and Row, 1977. This is an excellent discussion of different grading recording systems.

19. Lunneborg, Patricia W.: College grades: What do professors intend to communicate to whom? Educational Assessment Center, Univ Wash at Seattle, June, 1977. (Multilithed.) Also appeared in AAUP Bull, March, 1978, 33-35.

20. Nathin, Eugene, and Guild, Robert: Evaluation of preclinical laboratory performance: A systematic study. J Dent Educ, 31(2): 152-161, 1967.

2

The Myth of Objectivity

1. Starch, D., and Elliott, E. C.: Reliability of grading high school work in English. School Rev, 20: 442-457, 1912.

    ____: Reliability of grading work in history. School Rev, 21: 676-681, 1913.

    ____: Reliability of grading work in mathematics. School Rev, 21: 254-259, 1913.

2. Hartog, P., and Rhodes, E. C.: An Examination of Examinations. London, Macmillan, 1935; The Marks of Examiners. London, Macmillan, 1936. Cited in Rowntree, Derek: Assessing Students: How Shall We Know Them? NY, Harper and Row, 1977.

3. Boulding, Kenneth: In praise of inefficiency. Graduate Woman, July/August, 1979, 29.

4. Haglund, Keith: Taking the National Boards to court (Well, almost). The New physician, 29(3): 32-33, 1980.

5. Teaching faculty in academe: 1972. Chron Higher Educ, August 27, 1973, 4.

6. Umstattd, J. G.: Teaching Procedures. Austin, Tex, The University Cooperative Society, 1954.

7. Spencer, Richard E., and Stallings, William: The Improvement of College Level Student Achievement Through Changes in Classroom Examination Procedures. Final Report Program No. 6-1174, USOE. Urbana, Univ Ill, November, 1970.

8. Van Buren, Abigal: Dear Abby: Test result "false-positive." Copyright, 1980. Reprinted with permission of Universal Press Syndicate. All Rights Reserved.

9. Watson, Richard A., and Tang, D. B.; The predictive value of prostatic acid phosphatase as a screening test for prostatic cancer. New Eng J Med, 303 (9): 501, 1980.

10. Bursztagn, Harold, Feinbloom, Richard I., Hamm, Robert M., and Brodsky, Archie: Medical Choices, Medical Chances. NY, Delacorte, 1981, p. xv.

3

Influencing Learning

1. Terry, Paul W.: How students study for three types of objective tests. Educ Res, 27: 333-343, 1934. (P. 343.)

2. Douglass, H. R., and Talmadge, M.: How university students prepare for new types of examinations. School and Society, 39: 318-320, 1934.

3. Meyer, George: An experimental study of the old and new types of examination: I. The effect of the examination set on memory. J Educ Psych, 25: 641-661, 1934.

W. H. FREEMAN & CO.

Moran, Joseph M., Morgan, Michael D., and Wiersma, James H.: Instructor's Guide for Introduction to Environmental Science. SF, Freeman, copyright 1980. Questions #8 (p. 16) and #9 (p. 6), used by permission of W. H. Freeman & Company.

HARPER & ROW

Faranda, Thomas W. and Prough, George E.: Test Bank to accompany McDaniel, Carl, Jr.: Marketing: An Integrated Approach. NY, Harper & Row, 1979. Question #13 (p. 89) reprinted by permission of the publisher.

Harner, Holt: Instructor's Manual and Test Items to accompany Goldsby: Biology, 2nd ed. NY, Harper & Row, 1979. Questions #17 (p. 30) and #18 (p. 111) reprinted by permission of the publisher.

Myers, Ellen Howell: Instructor's Manual to accompany Garraty, John A.: The American Nation: A History of the United States Since 1865, 4th ed. NY, Harper & Row, 1979. Questions #1 (p. 166), #5 (181), and #22 (170) reprinted by permission of the publisher.

HOUGHTON MIFFLIN

Bell, Martin, L.: Instructor's Manual to Marketing: Concepts and Strategy, 3rd ed. Boston, Houghton Mifflin, 1979. Questions #2 (p. 81) and #12 (p. 6) used by permission of Houghton Mifflin Company.

ALFRED A. KNOPF

Weitz, Charles: Resource Manual for Jolly, Clifford, J., and Plog, Fred: Physical Anthropology and Archeology. NY, Knopf, 1976. Question #3 (p. 60) used by permission of Alfred A. Knopf, Inc.

MACMILLAN

Aufmuth, Beth: Instructor's Supplement to Denisoff, R. Serge, and Wahrman, Ralph: An Introduction to Sociology, 2nd ed. NY, Macmillan, 1979. Questions #10 (p. 101), #11 (p. 78), #23 (p. 111), #24 (p. 111), #26 (p. 23), #27 (p. 86), #28 (p. 87), #29 (p. 105), and #30 (p. 116) reprinted with permission of Macmillan Publishing Co.

Herreid, Clyde F., II: Instructor's Manual for Biology. NY, Macmillan, 1977. Questions #6 (p. 67) and #7 (p. 68) reprinted with permission of Macmillan Publishing Co.

Where To?

1. Blackburn, Robert T., Pellino, Glenn R., Boberg, Alice, and O'Connell, Colman: Are instructional programs off-target? Current Issues in Higher Education, No. 1, 1980. AAHE, Washington, DC 20036.

2. The best non-legal discussion of this case and related educational issues is the paper by Sheila Huff: Credentialing by tests or by degrees: Title VII of the Civil Rights Act and Griggs v. Duke Power Company. Harv Educ Rev, No. 2, 1974.

3. McBeth, Paul E., Jr., et al. vs. Dr. Monty Elliott, et al. Circuit Court of Oregon for Jackson County, 1978.

4. Bloom, Benjamin S.: Changing conceptions of examining at the University of Chicago. In Dressel, Paul L.: Evaluation in General Education. Dubuque, Iowa, Brown, 1954.

5. Swarthmore College Faculty: An Adventure in Education. NY, Macmillan, 1941.

6. THE TEST has a long and vague history. I encountered it through Vernon A. Nelson, Lieutenant Colonel, United States Air Force. He had received it years earlier from one of his students.

Appendix A

Grades and Reliabilities

Estimated Percentages of Incorrect Marking on the Basis of Measures of Differing Degrees of Reliability, Assuming a Five-Category (5-25-40-25-5) Distribution

Reliability of Measures	Percent Incorrect
1.00	0
0.99	5
0.98	9
0.95	15
0.90	23
0.80	33
0.70	40
0.50	50
0.00	70

This is table 15.6 from Robert L. Ebel, <u>Essentials of Educational Measurement</u> 1972, p. 426. Reprinted by Permission of Prentice-Hall, Inc., Englewood Cliffs, N.J.

Answers to THE TEST:

1. d; 2. b; 3. a; 4. a; 5. c; 6. b

Appendix B

Useful Books About Tests

These books have been selected in the hope that altogether they address the primary issues and concerns that most readers have about educational tests.

Berk, Ronald A. (Ed.). CRITERION-REFERENCED MEASUREMENT: THE STATE OF THE ART. Baltimore, Hopkins, 1980.

"Criterion-referenced" is a term becoming much in vogue and while it is not new to testing specialists, it is new for the general public. This book is a comprehensive assessment of that concept.

* * * * *

Burns, Edward. THE DEVELOPMENT, USE AND ABUSE OF EDUCATIONAL TESTS. Springfield, Ill., Thomas, 1979.

Designed for both teachers and lay persons, this book goes beyond details of classroom testing and examines and clarifies broad issues such as the potentials of testing. Educational testing is demystified.

* * * * *

Ebel, Robert L. ESSENTIALS OF EDUCATIONAL MEASUREMENT. Englewood Cliffs, N.J., Prentice-Hall, 3d edition, 1979.

This book of some 400 pages of text in 19 chapters is sound, very readable, and practical. The technical points only touched on in the present volume, such as reliability and validity, are elaborated clearly therein. There is a glossary of the terms and concepts used in educational measurement.

* * * * *

Gronlund, Norman E. CONSTRUCTING ACHIEVEMENT TESTS. Englewood Cliffs, N.J., Prentice-Hall, 2d edition, 1977 (paper).

A basic theme of this very practical guide is that classroom testing should support and reinforce other instructional activites--with all of them being designed to improve learning. The writing is direct and easily understood; suggestions are illustrated liberally by sample test items.

* * * * *

McCall, William A. HOW TO MEASURE IN EDUCATION. NY, Macmillan, 1927.

Note the publication date of this book--1927. It is being mentioned here for historical interest. Also, some of the testing concepts being ignored in classrooms today came into being at least 50 years ago.

* * * * *

Mager, Robert F. PREPARING INSTRUCTIONAL OBJECTIVES. Belmont, Calif., Fearon, 2d edition, 1975.

While the contents of this small paperback seem deceptively simple, the substance is profound, especially for those who have given little thought to course objectives. The writing is witty and clever.

* * * * *

Rowntree, Derek. ASSESSING STUDENTS: HOW SHALL WE KNOW THEM? NY, Harper and Row, 1977.

This book is more philosophical than technical. The purposes of assessment or evaluation are questioned, its effects on teacher-student relationships are examined, and questions are asked about the qualities it does and should identify. This is one of the most thoughtful pieces I have encountered and it covers the gamut from the early grades on. The discussions about grade recording practices will be helpful to all.